Conversational
English-Tibetan Dictionary

Bibliotheca Indo-Buddhica Series No.-115

Conversational
English-Tibetan Dictionary

Compiled by
Anil Gupta

Sri Satguru Publications
A Division of
Indian Books Centre
Delhi, India

Published by
Sri Satguru Publications,
Indological and Oriental Publishers
A Division of
Indian Books Centre
40/5, Shakti Nagar,
Delhi-110007
India

Email: ibcindia@ibcindia.com
Website: http://www.ibcindia.com/

First Edition: Delhi, 1992
Reprinted; Delhi, 1999

ISBN 81-7030-352-4

Published by Sunil Gupta for Sri Satguru Publications, a division of Indian Books Centre, 40/5, Shakti Nagar, Delhi-110007, India and printed at Mudran Bharti. Delhi-110 007

A

A, An, art *chi.*

Aback *gyap-lo-la.*

Abaft *shu-la.*

Abandon, to *shak-pa; pany wa.*

Abate, to (in price) *chak-pa.*

Abbot *khen-po.*

Abbreviate, to *du-pa; dum, dum che-pa.*

Abdomen *do-kho.*

Abhess *a-ni um-dze.*

Abide, to *dc-pa.*

Ability *wang.*

Abject *duk-po.*

Able, adj *khe-po.*

Able-bodied *top chhem-po.*

Ablution *thru.*

Abode *khang-pa; nang.*

Abolish, to *me-pa so-wa.*

Abominable *kyuk-tro-po.*

Abortion *pu-gu shor-wa.*

About (approximately) *tsa.*

About (concernig) *ton-la; kor-la.*

Above (higher up a hill) *ya-la.*

Above (on top of) *teng la; gang-la.*

Abridge, to *du-pa.*

Abruptly *lam-sang.*

Abscess *shu-wa.*

Absent, to be *me-pa.*

Absence *me-to.*

Absolutely (used negatively) *be te, khyon-ne.*

Absolve, to *sel-wa.*

Abstain from, to *pang wa.*

Absurd, to be *ton-ta me-pa.*

Abundant *be-po; dzak-to.*

Abuse, s. *me-ra.*

Abuse, to *me-ra tang-wa.*

Abyss *yang-sar-po.*

Accept, to *lem-pa.*

Access, to have *dro-chhok-pa; chhin-chhok-pa.*

Accident *par-chhe.*

Accommodation *shong-sa.*

Accompany, to *nyam-tu yong-wa.*

Accomplice *ro.*

Accomplished, to be (completed) *tshar-wa.*

According to *nang.*

Account *tsi.*

Account Book *tsi-tho.*

Account of, on *kyen-kyi.*

Accountant *tsi-pa.*

Accounts, to do *tsi-gyap-pa.*

Accumulate, to (money) *sak-pa.*

Accurate *thrik-thrik; ten-ten.*

Accusation *nye.*

Accuse, to *nye tsuk-pa.*

Accustomed, to be *kom-pa.*

Ache, s. *suk.*

Ache, to *na-wa.*

Achieve, to *che-pa.*

Acid *kyur-po.*

Aconite *tsen tu.*

Acquaintance (friend) *ngo-shem-pemi.*

Acquainted, to be *ngo shem-pa.*

Acquainted, to get *ngo she tang-wa.*

Acquire, to *jor-wa; thop-pa.*

Acquirement (skill) *yon-ten.*

Acquit, to *lo-pa; tang-wa.*

Acquitted, to be (in a case) *tang-shak-pa.*

Across *pha.*

Act, to *che-pa.*

Action (law suit) *kham-chhu.*

Active *hur-po.*

Actor *a-chhe-hla-mo.*

Actress *a-chhe-hla-mo.*

Actual *ngo-tho.*

Acute (knife) *no-po.*

Adage *tam-pe.*

Adams-apple *ok-dom.*

Add, to *nom-be tre-pa.*

Additional *non-ke.*

Adequate, to be *drik-pa.*

Adhere, to *jar-wa.*

Adieu (to a person departing) *ka-le phe.*

Adjourn, to *shak-pa.*

Adjust, to *drik-pa.*

Admiration *mo-pa.*

Admire, to *mo-pa che-pa.*

Admire, to (things) *sem-shor- wa.*

Admittance, to grant *je-kha nang-wa.*

Admonish, to *lap-cha che-pa.*

Admonition *lap-cha.*

Adopted child *so-thruk.*

Adore, to *mo-ku che-pa.*

Adorn, to *gyen-chha tak-pa.*

Adornment *gyen-chha.*

Adrift, to be *chhu-gang-lading-wa.*

Adroit *tse-chhem-po.*

Adult *lo-tar-ma; shom-pa.*

Adulterate, to *dre-tang-wa.*

Adulterer *chhe-po.*

Adulteress *chhe-mo.*

3

Advance (of money)   *ngam-chhi.*

Advantage   *phen; phen-tho.*

Adversary   *dra.*

Advice   *tro.*

Advice to ask   *tro-tri-wa.*

Advice, to give   *tro-che-pa.*

Aerogramme   *nam-dag yi-koe.*

Aeroplane   *nam-tru.*

Affair (Business)   *le-ka; ton-ta.*

Affection   *cham-po.*

Affectionate, to be   *cham-po che-pa.*

Affirm, to   *lap-pa.*

Affix, s.(grammatical)   *jen-ju.*

Affix, to   *drel-a.*

Afflicted, to be   *ka-le chung wa.*

Affliction   *ka-le.*

Afford, to   *ter-wa.*

Affray, to commit an   *lak-dzing che-pa.*

Afloat, to be   *chhu-gang-la yang-wa.*

Afoot (on foot)   *kang-thang-la.*

Afraid, to be   *she-pa.*

After   *shu-la; je-la.*

After noon   *gong-ta.*

After wards   *shu-la; je-la.*

Again   *yang-kyar.*

Against, over   *kha-thu-la.*

Age (of a human being)   *lo.*

Age (of an animal)   *na.*

Aged, m.   *ga-pu.*

Agent   *le-tshap.*

Aggravated, to be (angry)   *tshik-pa sa-wa.*

Agile   *hur po.*

Agitate, to (shake)   *truk-pa.*

Agitated, to be   *sem tshap-pa.*

Agony   *du-nge.*

Agree. to   *drik-pa; chhampa.*

Agreeable   *thum po.*

Agreeable (in taste)   *shim po.*

Agreement (bond)   *kam-gya.*

Agriculture   *so-nam.*

Agriculturist   *so-nam che-khen.*

Ague   *tshe-ne.*

Ague, to have   *dar-gyap-pa.*

Ahead (in front)   *ngen-la.*

Aid   *ro.*

Aid, to   *ro-che-pa.*

Ail, to   *na-wa.*

Ailment   *na-tsha.*

Air (atmospheric wind)   *hlak-pa; lung.*

Air (mien)   *dang : aong.*

Air mail   *nam-dag.*

Alarm, to   *she-tra lang-wa.*

Alas   *a-kha-kha.*

Alert   *chang-po.*

Alien   *chho-mi.*

Alight to (from horse)   *pap pa.*

Alight to be (of fire)   *bar wa.*

Alike   *chik-pa.*

Alive, to be   *som-po yo-pa.*

All day   *nyin-kang.*

All right   *la-so; la-la-si.*

All-wise   *tham-che khyempa.*

Alliance (relation)   *gyu-tsa.*

Allied, to be   *kha-thum-pa.*

Allot, to   *go pa.*

Allotment (share allotted)   *ke-la.*

Allow, to   *chuk-pa.*

Alloy   *hle.*

Allure, to   *lu-wa.*

Almanack   *da-tho; le-tho.*

Almighty   *ku-wang chhempo.*

Almond   *gya-kar tar-ka.*

Almost   *ha-lam.*

Alms   *jim-pa.*

Alms to give   *jim-pa tang-wa.*

Alms, to ask   *long-wa.*

Alone   *chik-po.*

Along with   *tang-nyam-tu.*

Aloud   *ke-chhem-po gyap-ne.*

Alphabet   *ka-kha.*

Already   *ta-ki-ne.*

Alright   *dig-zhaa.*

Also   *yang.*

Altar   *chho-sham.*

Alter, to (fit of clothes)   *sop-cho ggyappa.*

Alternately   *no-me che-ne.*

Although   *kyang; rung na; yan.*

Altogether (in total)   *tham-che dom ne.*

Alum   *kyu-mu-tsha.*

Aluminium   *ha-yang.*

Always   *nam-gyun; tu gyun.*

Am   *yo.*

Amass, to   *du-pa.*

Amaze, to   *yam-tshen che-pa.*

Amazement   *yam-tshen.*

Amazing   *yam-tshem-po.*

Ambassador   *ku-tshap.*

Amber   *po-she.*

Ambition   *thon-do.*

Ambitious   *thon-du chhempo.*

Amble (of a horse)   *dro.*

Ambling pony   *dro-ma.*

Amend. to   *so-kyor che-pa.*

Amendment   *shu-ta.*

Amicable   *thum-po.*

Amicable relationship (state of)
                    thun lam.

Amidst   *kyi-la.*

Ammunition   *dzen-de.*

Among   *kyi-la.*

Among ourselves   *nang-tsa.*

Amount, total   *khyon-dom.*

Ample   *mang-po.*

Amusement   *tse mo.*

Amusement, to have   *thu-tro
                    tang-wa.*

Analogy   *pe.*

Ancestry   *ri-gyu; mi-gyu.*

Ancestry of lama   *dung-dyu.*

Anchor   *ting-do.*

Ancient   *ngon-kyi.*

Anciently   *ngon-la; ngon tu.*

And   *yang; tang.*

Anecdote   *drum.*

Angel   *pho-nya.*

Angel (corner)   *sur.*

Anger   *tshik-pa khony-thro.*

Angry, to be   *tshik-pa sa-wa;
                    khongthro sa-wa.*

Angular   *sur-many-po yo pa.*

Animal   *sem-chem.*

Animal (wild)   *ri-ta.*

Ankle   *bol-gong.*

Annals   *lo-gyu.*

Annals (of kings)   *gye-rap.*

Annihilate, to   *tham-che me-pa
                    so-wa.*

Announce, to   *len-tre-pa;
                    len-kyel-wa.*

Annoy, to   *kong-thro lang.wa.*

Annoyed, to be   *tsher-wa.*

Annually   *lo-re-re.*

Anoint, to   *chuk-pa; ku-wa.*

Another   *shem-pa; yem-pa*

Answer, to   *len-gyap-pa.*

Answer, s   *len.*

Ant   *tro-ma.*

Antagonist   *dra.*

Antelope   *tso.*

Antique   *nying-pa*

Anus   *kup.*

Anvil   *ok-tsa.*

Anxiety   *sem-thre.*

Anxious, to be   *sem-thre che-pa.*

Any   *Kang yang.*

Anybody (with negative)   *su-kang;
                    su-yang.*

Anyhow (in any case)   *ka-rc
                    yin-ne yang*

Apartment   *khang-mik.*

Aperture   *gi-khung.*

Apo   *pe-u.*

Apologize, to   *thu-gong-ta shu-wa.*

Apology   *thu-gong-ta*

Apoplexy   *sa gyap-pa.*

Apothecary's shop   *men khang.*

Apparatus   *lak chha.*

Apparel   *chhu-pa.*

Appeal, to   *sh'u-wa.*

Appear, to (to be seen)   *thong-wa.*

Appear, to cause to (ghost, etc.)   *chen-dren shu wa.*

Appearance   *yip; sop-ta.*

Appetite   *tang-ka.*

Applaud, to   *to-ra tang-wa.*

Applause   *to-ra.*

Apple   *ku-shu.*

Application, written   *shu-yi.*

Apply, in writing, to   *shu-yi phu-wa.*

Apply, to   *nye-shu-phu-wa.*

Appoint, to (an officer)   *ku-wa.*

Approach, to (an object)   *dram-la dro-wa:dram-la yong-wa.*

Approve, to (sanction)   *ka-nang-wa.*

Appurtenance   *cha-la*

Apricot   *nga-rikham-bu.*

April   *chin-dha zhi-pa.*

Apron   *pang-den.*

Aqueduct   *yo po.*

Arbitrate, to   *par-mi che-pa.*

Archer   *da-pa.*

Ardnous   *ka-le- khak-po.*

Are   *yo : du; ve.*

Area   *gya.*

Argue, to   *tse-gyap-pa.*

Argument   *tso-pa.*

Arid   *kam-po.*

Arise, to   *lang-wa.*

Arithmetic   *tsi.*

Arm   *lag-ngar.*

Arm, upper   *lak-pe-nya.*

Arm-pit   *chhen-khung.*

Armful   *pany-ku-kang.*

Armlet   *dro-dung.*

Armour   *thrap.*

Arms (weapon)   *tshon-chha.*

Army   *mak-pung.*

Around   *khor la.*

Arouse, to (from sleep)   *nyi-se-pa.*

Arrange, to   *drik-pa.*

Arrest, to   *sim-pa.*

Arrive, to   *lep-pa.*

Arrogant   *nyam-chhem-po:*
            dza-kho chhem-po

Arrow   *da.*

Art, s.   *yon-ten.*

Artery   *tsa.*

Artful   *chang-po.*

Article   *cha-la; ngo ri.*

Artist (painter)   *hla-rina.*

As (like)   *nang-shin; dra-po.*

As far as   *par-tu; thu.*

Ascend, to   *dzak-pa.*

Ascent (uphill)   *kyen.*

Ascertain, to   *ha-ko-wa che-
                 pa.*

Ascetic   *gom-chhen.*

Ashamed   *ngo-tsha-po.*

Ashamed, to feel   *ngo-tsha-wa.*

Ashes   *ko-the.*

Aside   *sur-tu.*

Ask, to   *tri-wa.*

Asleep, to fall   *nyi-khuk-pa.*

Ass   *pung-ku.*

Assail, to   *rup-gyap-pa.*

Assassin   *mi-so-khen.*

Assassinate, to   *se-pa.*

Assault, to   *dung-wa.*

Assemble, to   *tshok-pa.*

Assembly-hall   *tshom-chhen.*

Assiduous   *tson-dru chhem-po.*

Assist, to   *ro-che-pa.*

Assistance   *ro.*

Assistant   *ro-che-khen.*

Associate   *ga-po nye-po.*

Associate, with to   *ga-po nyo-
                     po yo-pa.*

Aster   *ke-sang me-to.*

Asthma   *ug-saa na-tsha.*

Astonish, to   *yam-tshen che
                pa.*

Astonished   *yam-tshem-pa.*

Astonishment   *yam-tshem po*

Astonishment   *yam-tshem*

Astride, to put   *kyom-pa.*

Astrologer   *tsi-pa.*

Astrology   *kar-tsi.*

Astronomer   *tsi-pa.*

Astronomy   *kar-tsi.*

Asunder   *so-so.*

At   *la.*

At all (negatively)   *tsa-ne.*

At once   *lam-sang.*

Athletic   *tse-chhem-po.*

Atlas   *sap-thra.*

Attach, to   *gyap-pa.*

Attach, to (by sticking together)   *jar-
                                     wa.*

Attached, to be (love)   *sem chhak-pa.*

Attain, to   *jor-wa; thop-pa.*

Attempt   *tson-dru.*

Attend, to (before lama)   *kun-dun-la je-wa.*

Attend, to (heed)   *nyem-pa; amcho nyem-pa.*

Attend, to (servant on master)   *shap-chhi shu-wa.*

Attendant   *yok-po.*

Attendant, female   *yo mo.*

Attentive, to be   *hur-tha che-pa.*

August   *chin-dha gyay-pa.*

Aunt (Paternal)   *a ni.*

Auspicos (omens)   *tem-dre.*

Authentic   *ngo-ne; ngo-tho.*

Author   *tsom-khen.*

Authority   *wang.*

Authorize   *wang-tre=pa.*

Autumn   *ton-ka.*

Autumn fall   *ton-ka.*

Auxiliary troops   *gyam-non.*

Avalanche   *kang-ru.*

Avarice   *ham-pa.*

Avaricious   *ham-pa chhem-po.*

Avenge, to   *dra-len lok-pa.*

Avoid, to (a person)   *yo-wa; sur-ne dro-wa.*

Await, to   *guk-pa.*

Awake, to   *nyi-se-pa.*

Away   *pha.*

Awkward   *duk-ru.*

Axe   *ta-ri.*

Ay (yes)   *la-so; la-la-si; la-ong*

Azure   *ngom-po.*

B

Baby (of few months)   *man-ja.*

Baby (older)   *pu-gu chhung-chhung.*

Bachelor   *pho-hrang-nga.*

Back   *to-gey*

Back (behind in place)   *gyap-la.*

Back (of body)   *gyap.*

Backbite   *kha-tang-wa*

Backbone   *gel-tshig.*

Backside   *kup*

Backwards   *gyap-to-la*

Bad (wicked)   *ngem-pa; kyuk tro-po*

Badge   *ta.*

Bag (made of leather)   *kye-pa*

Bag (large)   *gye-mo*

Bag(small)   *phe-ko*

Baggage   *to-po.*

Bail   *khe-khya.*

Bail to   *khe-khya che-pa.*

Bake to   *pa-le trak-pa.*

Bakshish   *so-re.*

Balance   *hla-ma.*

Bald   *sang-kho.*

Bale   *to-po.*

Ball   *di-u.*

Ball cartridge   *dik-ri.*

Balloon   *lung-tru.*

Bamboo   *nyung-ma.*

Banana   *khe-dong.*

Band (gang of men)   *tsho.*

Band (hoop)   *shen.*

Bandages   *ma-tri.*

Bandit   *chak-pa.*

Bandy-legged   *kang-kyo.*

Banish, to   *gyam-phu tang-wa.*

Bank   *ngul-khang.*

Bank(of river)   *dram.*

Banker   *pun-da.*

Banner   *tar-chhar.*

Banquet   *drom-po.*

Baptism   *thru-so.*

Baptize, to   *thru-so nang-wa.*

Bar   *tum-pu.*

Bar   *chhang-khang.*

Barbarian   *tha-khop-pa.*

Barber   *ta zhar-khen.*

Bare(naked)   *ma-hrang-nga.*

Barefooted   *kang-je-ma.*

Bargain   *tshong.*

Bark   *pak-pa.*

Barley   *ney.*

Barley-flour   *tsam-pa.*

Barn   *dru-khang.*

Barrel (of gun)   *cha-hrang.*

Barren(of women)   *rap-chhe.*

Barrier (fence)   *ra-wa.*

Barter   *je-wa.*

Bashful, to be   *ngo-tsha-wa.*

Basin (for washing hands)   *tung-pen.*

Basket   *le-ko; le-po.*

Bat   *gam-po.*

Bath   *chhu-shong .*

Bathe, to   *thru-pa.*

Bathroom   *tru-khang.*

Battle   *ma.*

Bazaar   *throm.*

Bead   *thrang-ngapa.*

Beak   *chho-to.*

Beam small   *cham-shing.*

Beam, large   *dung-ma.*

Bean   *tre-ma.*

Bear   *tom.*

Bear , to (carry)   *khyer-wa.*

Beard   *ok-sho.*

Beast (of prey)   *chen-sen.*

Beat, to   *dung-wa.*

Beaten, to be   *pham-pa.*

Beautiful   *dze-po.*

Beaver   *chhu-tram.*

Because   *kyen-kyi; ton-la.*

Become, to   *chung-wa.*

Becoming   *o-po.*

Bed   *nyay-tri.*

Bedaub, to   *chuk-pa; ku-wa*

Bedding   *nye-sen*

Bedroom   *nye-sa.*

Bedsheet   *nyel-rey.*

Bee   *drang-ma.*

Bee-hive   *drang-tshang.*

Beef   *lang-sha.*

Beer   *chhang.*

Beer-shop   *chhang-ma; thrung-ma.*

Bees-wax   *trak-tshi.*

Beetle   *drang-pu.*

Beftting   *u-po.*

Beg, to (request)   *shu-wa.*

Beget, to   *kye-pa.*

Beggar   *pang-ko.*

Begin, to   *go-tsuk-pa.*

Beginning   *go.*

Beguile, to   *go-kor-wa.*

Behalf of, on   *ton-la.*

Behaviour   *che-tang.*

Belch, to   *gak-tri gyap-pa.*

Belief (religion)   *te-pa.*

Believe, to   *yi-chhe-pa.*

Bell   *tri-pu.*

Bell-metal   *li.*

Bellows   *bu-pa.*

Belly   *tro-kho; khok-pa.*

Belong , to(to me)   *yim-pa*

Belong(to you or third person)   *re-pa*

Beloved   *che-po.*

Below   *ma.*

Belt   *ke-ra.*

Bench   *kup-kya; thri-u-shing.*

Bend, to   *kuk-pa.*

Bend, to (stop)   *ku-ku che-pa.*

Beneath   *o-la.*

Benediction   *chin-lap*

Benefaction   *gon-dren*

Benefactor   *gon-dren nang-khen*

Benefit, to   *phen-thok-pa*

Benevolence   *trin.*

Benevolent   *trip-chhem-po.*

Bent, to be   *ku-ku che-ne de-pa.*

Beseech, to   *shu-wa phu-wa.*

Beside   *tsa-la.*

Besprinkle with water, to   *chhu-chha gyap-pa.*

Best   *yak-sho; yak-thak-chho.*

Bestow, to   *ter-wa*

Bet   *gyen.*

Betel-nut   *ko-yu*

Betray, to   *dra-i wang-la tang-wa*

Better   *yak-ka.*

Better, to get the   *gye-wa .*

Between   *pa-la.*

Beware, to   *tok-son che-pa.*

Beyond   *pha-chho-la.*

Bhutan   *druk-yu .*

Bhutanese   *druk-pa.*

Bible   *sung-rap.*

Bicycle   *kang-ga-ri.*

Bid, to   *ka-nang-wa*

Bier   *shing-thri*

Big   *chhem-po*

Bile   *thri-pa*

Bill (of bird)   *chho-to*

Bill (amount)   *tsi-tho*

Billow   *ba-lap.*

Bind, to   *dam-pa*

Biography   *nam-tha*

Birch tree   *tak-pa-shing*

Bird   *cha*

Bird's nest   *cha-tshang*

Bird-cage   *lung-tse*

Birth-place   *kye-sa; kye-se lung-pa.*

Birthday   *kye-tshe.*

Bishop   *khem-po.*

Bit (of a bridle)   *trap-cha.*

Bit (piece)   *tum-pu.*

Bitch   *khyi-mo.*

Bitter   *khak-thi.*

Black   *nag-po.*

Blacksmith   *gar-ra.*

Bladder   *gang-phu*

Blade (of sword)   *ngo*

Blame, to   *kyon lom-pa*

Blank   *long-pa*

Blanket   *kam-pa-li.*

Blaze, s   *me*

Blaze, to (of fire)   *bar-wa*

Bleat, to   *luk-ke gyap-pa*

Blessing(by laying hand on head)
            chhu-wang

Blind   *long-nga*

Blind of one eye   *mik-shar-ra*

Blink, to   *mik-tsum gyap-pa*

Blithe   *kyi-po*

Blockhead   *kuk-pa; lem-pa*

Blood   *traa.*

Blossom   *me-to*

Blouse   *won-joo.*

Blow (with fist)   *dzo-ram*

Blue   *ngon-po.*

Blue Book   *tep ngom-po*

Blunder, to   *kha-nor-wa*

Blunt, to be   *no-po me-pa*

Boar   *phak-pa*

Board   *pang-le*

Boast, to   *rang-to che-pa*

Boat   *tru*

Body   *zug-po.*

Boil   *nyen-bur.*

Boil (watery)   *chhu-pur*

Boiled   *khol-ma.*

Bold   *lo-kho chhem-po*

Bolt   *gon-cha*

Bolt, to (door)   *gon-cha gyap-pa*

Bond (for amount)   *kam-gya*

Bone   *rue-go.*

Book   *pe-chha*

Book written   *tri-ma*

Book, printed   *par-ma*

Book, language   *chho-tshi*

Boon   *trin*

Boots   *iham.*

Border   *sur*

Born, to be   *khe-wa*

Borrow , to   *yar-wa*

Bottle   *she-tam*

Bottom   *ting*

Bough   *ye-ka*

Bound, to (jump)   *chhong-pa;*
            chhong-gya gyap-pa

Boundary   *san-tsham*

Bountiful   *lak-pa shok-po*

Bow (for shooting)   *shu*

Bowel   *gyu-ma*

Bowl (for drinking water & tea)
            phor-pa

Boy   *pu-gu*

Bracelet   *dro-dung*

Brahma   *tshang-pa*

Brahman   *tram-se*

Brain   *le-pa.*

Branch   *ye-ka*

Brandy   *a-ra*

Brass   *raa.*

Brave   *nying-chhem-po.*

Bread   *baa-le.*

Break, to   *chak-pa*

Breakfast   *zhog-ja.*

Breast   *bang-kho nu-ma.*

Breathless, to be   *u sak-pa.*

Breed (of men)   *gyu.*

Breeze   *hlak-pa; lung.*

Bribe   *tsik-tho.*

Brick   *sa-pa.*

Bride   *na-ma.*

Bridegroom   *mak-pa.*

Bridesmaid   *pa-ro.*

Bridge   *sam-pa.*

Bridle   *trap.*

Brief   *thung-thung.*

Brier   *tsher-ma.*

Brigand   *chak-pa.*

Bright (clear)   *se-po.*

Brilliant   *o-chhem-po.*

Bring, to (by carrying)   *khyer-yong-wa*

Broad   *shang-chhem-po*

Broadcloth   *go-nam*

Broil   *gyam-dre*

Bronze   *li-ma.*

Brooch   *ke thru*

Broom   *chha-ma*

Broth   *khu-a*

Broth (made from meat)   *sha-khu*

Brother   *pun-kya*

Brother, elder   *cho-cho*

Brother, mother's   *a-shang*

Brother-inlaw (sister's husband)   *pun- kya ki khyo-ga*

Brother-inlaw (wife brother)   *kyi-men kyi pun-kya*

Brown   *gya-mug.*

Bruised, to be   *trak-pa*

Brush   *pha-se*

Brute   *cho-song*

Bubble   *bu-wa*

Buck   *sha-a*

Bucket   *chhu-som*

Buddha   *sang-gye*

Buddhist   *nang-pa*

Buffalo   *ma-he*

Buffoonery   *tre-lse*

Bug   *dre-shi*

Bugle   *mak tung*

Build, to   *so-wa*

Building   *khang-pa*

Bulk   *chhe-chhung*

Bulky   *bom-po*

Bull   *lang; lang-ko*

Bullet   *dik-ri*

Bullock   *lang; lang-ko*

Bunch   *chhak-pa*

Bundle of clothes   *ko-dril*

Bundle of papers   *shuk-ku-i chak-pa*

Burn, to   *tshik-pa*

Burrhel (sheep)   *na-wa*

Burst, to   *ke-pa*

Bush   *shing-dong chhung-chhung*

Business   *le-ka; ton-ta*

But   *yin-kyang; yin-na-yang*

Butcher   *shem-pa; ya-po*

Butler   *sim-pon*

Butt (of gun)   *gum-shing nya-shu*

Butter   *maa.*

Butter lamp   *chho-me.*

Butter-milk   *tar-ra*

Butterfly   *chhem-drem-ma*

Buttock   *kup*

Button   *thup-chhi*

Buy, to   *nyo-wa*

Buzz, to   *drang-ke gyap-pa*

By (reason of)   *kyen-kyi*

By (post)   *ki; kyi; kyi*

C

Cabbage   *lo-kho pe-tshay.*

Cage   *cha-thra*

Cairn   *do-pung*

Cake   *ten-shin*

Calculate, to   *tsi-gyap-pa*

Calculation   *tsi*

Calendar   *da-tho*

Cambric   *tar-re*

Camp   *gar*

Camphor   *ka-pur*

Camping ground   *ga-sa*

Canal   *yo-po*

Candid   *trang-po*

Candle   *yang-laa.*

Cane   *pa*

Cannibal   *mi-i-sha-sa*

Cannon-ball   *me-gyok-ki di-u*

Canter, to   *dzo-gyap-pa*

Cap   *sha-mo.*

Capable   *nu-po*

Capital(letters)   *u-chen*

Capital(as opposed to interest)   *ngo-po*

Capital(chief city) *gye-khap,*
gye-sa

Captive *tsom-pa*

Capture, to *sim-pa*

Carbon paper *nag-sho.*

Carcass *ro*

Card *yi-ge*

Cards, playing *shon*

Care, to take *ten-ten che-pa*

Career(manner of life) *che-tang*

Carefully *cha-ka che-ne*

Carpenter *shing-so-wa*

Carpet *sa-den*

Carriage *shing-ta khor-lo*

Carrier *to-po khyer-khen*

Carrot *gung-la-phuk.*

Carry, to *khyer-wa; khur-wa*

Cart, bullock *lang-ga-ri*

Cartridge *dik-ri*

Carve, to(on wood, iron) *tro-gyap-pa*

Case (law suit) *kham-chhu*

Case(box) *gam*

Cash *ngu*

Cashier *Chhan-dzo*

Caste *ru*

Castle *gyal-khang.*

Castrate, to *sha-che-pa*

Cat *shi-mi*

Cataract *ha-ri-long-nga*

Catch, to *sim-pa*

Catechu *to-ja*

Caterpillar *sa-bu*

Cattle *pa-lang*

Cattle-disease *chhu-ne*

Cauliflower *me-to pe-tshay.*

Cause (reason) *kyen; gyu-kyen*

Cave *daa-phu.*

Cave of rock *trak-phu*

Cavity *khog-tong.*

Cease, to *chhe-pa*

Ceaseless *gyun-mi-chhe-pa*

Ceiling *tho-kha*

Celebrated *nyen nyen-tra chhem-po*

Cemetery *tu-thro*

Censer *po-phor*

Centre *khi*

Centurion *gya-pon*

Ceremony *luk-so*

Ceremony(religious) *chho-ga; ku-rim*

Certain *nge-pa*

Certainly *ten-den; ngo-tho*

Certificate *ka-sho*

Chaff (of grain)	*phung-ma.*	Chest	*bang-kho.*
Chain, iron	*chak-tha*	Chicken	*ja-sha.*
Chair	*kup-kyaa.*	Chicken pox	*dhug-gyong bur.*
Chairman	*thri-pa*	Chide, to	*she-she tang-wa*
Chalk	*sa-kar; kar-tsi*	Chief minister	*lon-chhen*
Chamber	*khang-mi*	Chief(among official)	*tso-o*
Chance(luck)	*so-de*	Chiefly	*phe-chher*
Change, to (exchange)	*je-po gyap-pa*	Child	*pu-gu*
		Childeren	*pu pu-mo*
Chapel	*chho-khang*	Chilli	*si-pen.*
Chapter	*li-u*	Chilly	*trang-mo; si-po*
Character	*che-tang*	Chimney	*tu-khung*
Charge, to (price)	*kong lap-pa*	Chin	*me-le.*
Charitable	*ge sem chhem-po*	China (country)	*gya-na.*
Charity	*jim-pa; sonyom*	Chinese	*gya-mi*
Chase, to	*shuk-te chhim-pa*	Chinese language	*gya-ke*
Chasm	*ser-ka*	Chisel	*song*
Chat, to	*khap-le she-pa*	Choke, to	*lo-sup gyap-pa*
Cheap	*khe-po*	Cholera	*shel-kyug.*
Cheat, to	*go-kor tang-wa*	Cholers	*khuk-she*
Check, to (stop)	*kak-pa.*	Choose, to(select)	*dam-pa*
Cheek	*kho-tsho.*	Chop(mutton chop)	*luk-she tsi-ma*
Cheeky	*kyong-po*		
Cheerful, to be	*sem-ga-wa*	Chopper	*tshe-to*
Cheese	*chhu-ra*	Chopstick	*kho-tsi.*
Chemist	*men-tshong-pa*	Christ	*ma-shi-ka*
Chess	*mi-ma*	Chronicle	*lo-gyu*

Church	*chho-khang*	Clear (of glass)	*se-po*
Churn, s	*dong-mo*	Cleft	*se-ka*
Cicatrice	*ma-shu*	Clergy	*tra-pa*
Cinder (hot)	*men-da*	Clerk	*trung-yi*
Cipher(zero)	*le-kor*	Clever	*rik-pa chhem-po*
Circle	*go-kor*	Climate	*si-tro*
Circular	*kor-kor*	Climb, to	*dzak-pa*
Circumference	*gor-thik*	Cling, to	*ju-pa*
Circumstance	*kyen*	Cloak	*chhu-pa*
Citadel	*dzong*	Clock	*chhu-tsho-khor-lo*
City	*trong-khyer*	Cloisonne	*ku-ku-sha*
Civil	*she-sa*	Close fisted	*lak-pa tam-po*
Claim	*thop-ke*	Close to,	*tsa; tha-nye-po*
Clairvoyance	*ngon-she*	Close up(of flowers etc)	*kha-sum-pa*
Clamour	*u-dra*	Cloth, cotton	*re*
Clap, the hands to	*lak-pa dap-pa*	Cloth, woollen	*go-nam*
Clarified butter	*mar-khu*	Clothe, to	*kom-pa*
Clarionet	*gya-ling*	Clothes	*tu-lo*
Clasp, to	*khyu-pa*	Clothes, to puton	*tu-lo kom-pa*
Class (kind)	*rim-pa*	Cloud (in sky)	*trim-pa*
Class(in school)	*tre*	Cloudy, to be come	*thip-pa*
Claw	*der-mo*	Clove	*li-shi*
Clay	*dak-pa*	Clown	*wu-khor shu-khen*
Clean	*tsang-ma*	Clumsy	*duk-ru*
Clean, to (by sweeping)	*ke-gyap-pa*	Coagulate, to(of Blood, etc.)	*khyak-pa*
Cleansed (purified)	*tak-po*	Coal	*do-su*

Coarse	*tsup-po*		Comet	*tu-wa juk-ring*
Coast	*chhu-dram*		Comfortable	*kyi-po*
Coat	*kor.*		Comic	*ge-mo tro-po*
Cobbler	*ngop-so*		Command, comandment	*ka*
Cobweb	*dom-tha*		Command, to(give order)	*ka-nang-wa*
Cock	*cha-pho*			
Coconut	*be-ta.*		Commander	*mak-pon*
Code of law	*thrim-yi*		Commander in chief	*chin-da*
Coffer	*gam*		Commence.to	*go-tsuk-pa*
Coffin	*ro-gam*		Commencement	*tho-ma*
Coin	*tang-ka*		Commerce	*tshong*
Cold	*chham-pa.*		Commissary(delegate)	*tshap*
Cold water	*chhu dang-mo.*		Commit, to	*che-pa*
Colic	*gyu-ser*		Common	*khu-ma*
Collar	*kong-nga*		Companion	*ro*
Collarbone	*jing-tshig.*		Company(of persons)	*mi-tsho*
Colleague	*ro-che-khem*		Compare, to	*dur-wa*
Collect, to	*du-pa.*		Comparison	*pe*
Collect, to (wood)	*druk-pa.*		Compel, to	*u-tshu che-pa*
Colloquial (language)	*phe-ke*		Compelled, to be	*go-pa*
Colour	*tshon-tra.*		Compensate, to	*dro-song ter·wa*
Colt	*ti-ki*			
Column	*ka*		Compensation	*dro-song*
Comb	*tra-she*		Compete, to	*dur-wa*
Combat	*gyam-dre*		Competent	*o-po*
Come	*sho*		Competitor	*dur-khen*
Come back, to	*lo-yong-wa*		Compile, to	*drik-pa*

Complain, to (in writing)   *nye-shu phu-wa*

Complaint(petition)   *nye-shu*

Complete, to   *tshar-wa*

Complicated   *go-nyo tsha-po*

Compliment   *chham-bu*

Compose, to(writing)   *tsom-pa*

Compromise, to   *nang drik che-pa, par-dum che-pa*

Compulate, to   *gyo-wa.*

Computation   *tsi*

Concerning   *ton-la; kor-la*

Conch-shell   *tung*

Conduct, s   *che-tang*

Conduit(drain)   *yo-po*

Cone of clay(with figures of gods)   *tsha-tsha*

Confer, to (converse)   *tro-che-pa*

Conference   *tro*

Confess, to   *shak-pa*

Confide, to   *lo-te-che-pa.*

Confidence   *lo-te*

Confidential   *sang-wa*

Confine , to   *chuk-pa*

Confirm, to (statement etc.)   *ten-den che-pa*

Confiscate, to   *shung-she tang-wa.*

Conflict   *gyam-dre.*

Confounded, to be   *go-khor-wa; go-thom-pa.*

Confront, to   *rap-thro tang-wa.*

Confused, to be   *go-khor-wa.*

Confusion   *go-tro.*

Confusion (of speech)   *khan-jo.*

Congeal, to   *khyak=pa*

Congregate, to   *dzom-pa.*

Congregation   *tsho.*

Conjure up, to   *chen-dren shu=wa.*

Conjure, to   *mik-thru-tse-pa*

Conjure, to(implore)   *nen-ten shu-wa.*

Conjurer   *mik-thru tse-khen.*

Conjuring tricks   *mik-thru.*

Connect, to (join together)   *thu-pa.*

Conquer, to   *gye-wa.*

Conscience, to have a   *sang-ngen she-pa.*

Conscious, to be   *trem-pa.*

Consecrate, to   *rap-ne che-pa*

Consecration   *rap-ne*

Consent, to   *nyem-pa.*

Consequently   *tei-kyen che-ne.*

Consider, to   *sam lo tang-wa.*

Considerable number of, a   *mang-nyung nyom po-chi*

Console, to	*sem-so tang-wa.*	Controversy	*tso-pa.*
Consonant, s.	*se-che.*	Convenant	*kha-ten; kha-chhe.*
Conspicuous	*ngon-se chhem po.*	Convent	*a-ni-: gom-pa.*
		Conversation	*ke-chha.*
Constable	*ko-chak-pa.*	Converse, to	*ke-chha che-pa.*
Constant	*tem-po*	Convex	*bur-bur.*
Constellation	*za-ka.*	Convey, to	*kye-wa.*
Constipation	*tsa-gak pa.*	Convulsions (of baby, etc.)	*ge-ser gyap-pa.*
Construct, to	*so-wa.*		
Consult, to	*tro-tri-wa.*	Cook	*ma-chhen*
Consume	*chhe*	Cookroom	*thap-tshang.*
Consumed, to be	*dzok-pa.*	Cool	*trang-mo; si-po.*
Consumption	*chong-ne.*	Cooly (carrier of load)	*to-pokhyer-khen; mi-hrang.*
Contamination	*trip*	Cooly (labourer)	*ar-po*
Contemplate, to	*sam-lo tang-wa.*	Copious	*mang-po; be-po.*
Contemporary	*lon-da.*	Copper	*zang.*
Contend, to	*ma-gyap-pa.*	Coppersmith	*sang-so-wa.*
Continent, s.	*ling*	Copy	*pe.*
Continually	*nam-gyun; tu-gyun*	Copy, true	*ngo-shu*
		Coral	*ju-ru.*
Contract, a large written	*kam-gya*	Cord	*thak-pa.*
		Cork (lid)	*khap-cho.*
Contractor	*pok-dzin-pa.*	Corn (grain)	*dru.*
Contradictory	*gyam-ge.*	Corner	*sur*
Contrite, to be	*gyo-pa kye-pa.*	Corpse	*ro.*
Contrition	*gyo-pa.*	Corpulent	*gyap-pa.*
Control	*wang.*	Correct	*dra-tak-po.*

Correction   *shu-ta.*

Correctly   *dra-tak-po che-ne.*

Corrupt, to   *me-pa so-wa nang-wa.*

Cost   *kong.*

Costly   *kong-chhem-po*

Cotton   *ting-bel.*

Cotton-cloth   *re-ko; re-chha.*

Cotton-thread   *re-ku.*

Cotton-wool.   *trim-pe.*

Cotton-yarn   *sing.*

Couch   *kup-kya; thri-u-shing*

Cough   *lo.*

Cough, to   *lo-gyap-pa.*

Council, Head   *ka-sha hlen-gye.*

Counsel   *tro.*

Count, to   *trang-ka gyap-pa.*

Countenance   *dong.*

Counterfeit, adj.   *ma-pin.*

Counting   *trang-ka.*

Country   *lung-pa.*

Country-House   *shi-ka.*

Couple, (a pair)   *chha.*

Courier   *pang-chhen.*

Court (of justice)   *thrim-khang.*

Court yard   *go-ra.*

Cousin   *pun kya.*

Cover   *khap-cho.*

Cover, to   *kap-pa.*

Covering   *khep.*

Covet, to   *ham-pa che-pa.*

Covetous   *ham pa chhem-po.*

Covetousness   *ham-pa.*

Cow   *pa.*

Coward   *sem-chhung-chhung*

Cowherd   *drok-pa.*

Cowry   *drom-pu.*

Cowshed   *pa-ra.*

Crab   *dik-sing.*

Crack, to v.i.   *ke-pa.*

Crafty   *yo-chhem-po.*

Cramp   *tsa-khum-pa.*

Crane (bird)   *cha-thrung-thrung.*

Crawl, to   *kha-pu kok-pa.*

Crazy   *nyom-pa.*

Cream   *kya-ser.*

Create, to   *ko-pa.*

Credible   *o-pa.*

Credit, to   *yi-chhe-pa.*

Creditor   *pun-da.*

Creed   *te-pa.*

Creek (in a lake)   *tsho-la*

Creep, to   *ka-pu kok-pa*

Crevice   *se-ka*

Crime, to commit   *thrim gel-wa.*

Criminal, adj.   *dzap-chhen.*

Crimson   *mar-po.*

Crippled   *kang-kyo.*

Crocodile   *chhu-sin*

Crooked (with one bend)   *ku-ku.*

Crop (of corn etc.)   *ton-tho.*

Cross of wood   *gyang shing.*

Cross, to   *gel-wa*

Cross-legged   *kyi-trum.*

Crow, s   *kha-ta.*

Crowd, s   *tshok.*

Crown of the head   *chi-tsu.*

Crucify, to   *gyang-shing-la kyang-wa.*

Cruel, to be   *nying-je me-pa.*

Crupper   *me.*

Crush, to   *dzi-wa*

Cry, to (weep)   *ngu-wa*

Crystal   *she.*

Cub of fox   *wa-thru.*

Cubit   *thru*

Cuckoo   *khu-yu*

Culprit   *dzap-chhen*

Cultivate, to   *shing-le che-pa.*

Cultivation   *so-nam.*

Cultivator   *so-nam che-khen.*

Cunning   *chang-po*

Cup   *ka-yol.*

Cup (earthenware)   *ka-yo.*

Curds   *sho.*

Cure, to   *trak-pa so-wa.*

Cured, to be   *trak-pa*

Curious   *khye-tshar-po*

Curly   *su-lu.*

Current   *chhu-gyun*

Curse, to   *mo-mo guop-pa.*

Curtail, to   *nyung-ru tang-wa.*

Curtain   *yo-la.*

Curve, to   *kuk-ku che-pa.*

Curved   *kuk-ku.*

Cushion   *den.*

Cushion (small placed on chair)   *kha-den.*

Custody   *tsi.*

Custom   *luk-so.*

Customs   *sho-thre.*

Cut   *cha.*

Cut, to   *che-pa.*

Camphor   *ka-pur*

Camping ground   *ga-sa*

Canal   *yo-po*

Candid   *trang-po*

Candle   *yang-laa.*

Cane *pa*

Cannibal *mi-i-sha-sa*

Cannon-ball

D

Dacoit *chak-pa.*

Dagger *am-tri; ga-so.*

Daily *nyi-ma tak-pa ri-shi.*

Dainty *yak-po.*

Dairy-farm *drok sa.*

Dalai Lama *kyam-gon rin po chhe;*

Dale *lung.*

Dam, s. (for water) *chhu-ra.*

Damage *kyon.*

Damp *lom-pa.*

Damsel *pu-mo.*

Dance *shap-ro.*

Dandy *gyo-chang.*

Danger *nyen.*

Dangerous *nyen-ka chhem-po*

Dare, to *nu-pa.*

Daring *nying-chhem-po.*

Dark *nak-po.*

Darkness *min-na.*

Darling *nying-du.*

Darn, to *tro-tuk gyap-pa.*

Dart *da.*

Date *tshe-pa.*

Daub, to *ku-wa.*

Daughter *pu-mo.*

Daughter *bu-mo.*

Daughter-in-law *na-ma.*

Dawn, s. *nam-lang.*

Day *nyi-ma.*

Day after tomorrow. *nang.*

Day before yesterday *khe-nyi-ma*

Day break *nam lang.*

Dazzling *o-chhem-chhem.*

Dead *ro.*

Dead, is *shi-song.*

Deaf *om-pa.*

Deal, a great *dzak-to.*

Dealer *tshong-po*

Dear (beloved) *che-po.*

Debar, to *kak-pa.*

Debate, to *tso-pa gyap-pa.*

Debt *pu-lon.*

Debtor *pu-lon len-khen.*

Decapitate, to *ke-che-pa.*

Decay, to *rul.*

Deceased, the *shi-khen.*

Deceit *go.*

Deceitful   *yo-chen; lo kyok-kyok.*

Deceive , to   *go-kor tang-wa.*

December   *Chin-dha; Chu-nyi*

Decent (becoming)   *o-po.*

Deception   *yo-gyu.*

Decide, to (judge)   *tha-che-pa.*

Decidedly   *thak-chho.*

Deciever   *9- kor tong. khen.*

Declare, to   *she-pa.*

Declivity   *thur.*

Decorate, to   *gyen-chha tak-pa.*

Decoration   *gyen-chha.*

Decrease, to (in numbers)   *nyung-ru chhim-pa.*

Decree (of court of justice)   *ka-thrim.*

Decrepit   *khok-pa.*

Dedicate, to   *ram-ne che-pa.*

Dedication   *ram-re.*

Deduct, to   *them-pa.*

Deed   *le-ka.*

Deep   *ting-ring-po.*

Deer   *sha.*

Deface, to   *sup-pa.*

Defamation   *me-ra.*

Defame, to   *me-ra tang-wa.*

Defeat, to   *gye-wa.*

Defect   *kyon.*

Defective   *kyon-chhem-po.*

Defend, to   *kyap-pa; kyong-wa.*

Defendant   *shu-tuk che-pe khap-the.*

Defer, to   *pu-ru shak-pa.*

Deficient   *chhe pa.*

Defile, to   *tsok-pa so-wa.*

Defilement   *trip.*

Define, to   *ton-ta she-pa.*

Definite (certain)   *nge-pa; ten-ten.*

Definitely   *ten-ten che-ne.*

Deformed, to be   *wang-po ma-tshang-wa.*

Defraud, to   *go-kor tang-wa.*

Degenerate, to   *nyam-pa.*

Degrade, to   *ko-ne pap-pa.*

Degree (series)   *rim-pa.*

Degrees, by   *rim-shin.*

Deity   *hla.*

Dejected, to be   *mi...ga-wa.*

Delay   *gor-po.*

Delay, to   *gor-po che-pa.*

Delay, without   *gor-po ma-che-par.*

Delegate   *tshap*

Deliberate, to   *tro-che-pa.*

Delicate (weak), to be   *thang-po me-pa.*

Delicious   *shim-thak-chho.*

Delight   *ga-tshor.*

Delight in, to take   *ga-wa.*

Deliver, to (give)   *tre-pa.*

Deliver, to (rescue)   *kyap-pa; kyong-wa.*

Deliverance   *thar-pa.*

Delude, to   *go-kor tang-wa.*

Deluge (flood)   *chhu-ru.*

Demand, to   *go-ser-wa.*

Demeanour   *che-tang.*

Demented   *nyom-pa.*

Demi-god   *lha-ma-yin*

Demolish, to   *shik-pa.*

Demon   *dong-dre; du.*

Den   *tshang.*

Denomination   *chho-lu*

Dense   *thuk-po.*

Dentist   *so'iem-ji.*

Deny, to   *gyam-ge cke-pa.*

Depart, to   *thom-pa; chhim-pa.*

Departed (deceased)   *shi-khen.*

Depend upon, to   *lo-kel-wa.*

Deportment   *che-tang.*

Deposit, to   *shak-pa.*

Depositary   *dzo.*

Depraved adj.   *duk-ru.*

Deprive, to   *throk-pa.*

Depth   *ting-ring-thung.*

Depute, to (send)   *tshap-tang-wa.*

Deputy   *tshap.*

Derangement   *kyon.*

Descend, to   *pap-yong-wa (or dro-wa.)*

Descendants   *ri-gyu; mi-gyu.*

Descent   *thur.*

Describe, to   *she-pa.*

Desert, s.   *che-thang.*

Deserve, to   *o-pa.*

Design (sketch)   *ri-mo.*

Design, to (copy)   *pe tri-pa.*

Desire, s.   *do-pa.*

Desist, to   *pang-wa.*

Despair, to   *yi-muk-po che-pa.*

Despatch, to   *tang-wa.*

Desperate, to be (hopeless)   *lo-tha che-pa.*

Despise, to   *ma-bep che-pa.*

Despondent, to be   *sem-kyo-wa*

Destiny (fate)   *so-de.*

Destitute   *kang-yang me-pa.*

Destroy, to	*me-pa so-wa.*
Detail, in	*ship po.*
Detailed, account	*tho*
Detain, to	*kak-pa.*
Determine, to	*tha-che-pa.*
Detest, to	*dra-che-pa.*
Device,	*chu.*
Devil	*dong-dre; du.*
Devotee (hermit)	*tsham-pa; gom-chhen.*
Devotion (faith)	*te-pa.*
Devour, to	*ha-phe ho-phe sa-wa.*
Devout,	*chho-sem chhem-po.*
Dew	*si-pa.*
Dexterous	*chang-po.*
Diadem	*cho-pen*
Dialect	*ke-lu.*
Diamond	*do-je pha-lam.*
Diarrhoea	*shel-ney.*
Dice, to play at	*sho-gyap-pa.*
Dictionary	*tshig-zo.*
Die, Dice, s.	*sho.*
Die, to	*shi-wa.*
Die, to (of great Lama)	*ku-shing-la phe-pa*
Diet	*kha-la; top-chhe.*
Difference	*khye; he-pa.*
Different	*mi-chik-pa.*
Difficult	*ka-le khak-po.*
Dig, to	*ko-wa.*
Digest, to	*ju-wa.*
Dignity	*ko-sa; ko-ne.*
Dilate, to	*kha-chhe-wa.*
Dilatory	*nya-si gu-si.*
Diligence	*nying-ru.*
Diligence, to use	*nying-ru che-pa.*
Diligent	*nying-ru chhem-po.*
Diligently	*nying-ru che-ne.*
Dim	*hrap-hrip.*
Dimension	*chhe-chhung.*
Diminish, to (in number)	*nyung-ru dro-wa.*
Dinner	*gong-dhaa kha-laa.*
Dip, to (into water, &c.)	*chuk-pa.*
Diploma	*ka-sho.*
Direction	*chho.*
Directly	*lam sang.*
Dirt	*tsok-pa.*
Dirt (mud)	*dzap.*
Dirty	*tsok-pa.*
Disadvantageous, to be	*phen-tho me-pa.*
Disagree, to	*mi thum-pa.*
Disappear, to	*ye-wa.*

Disbelieve, to   *yi mi chhe-pa.*

Disc   *khor-lo.*

Discharge, to (dismiss)   *gong-pa ter-wa.*

Discharge, to (fire off)   *gyap-pa.*

Discharge, to (free)   *tang-wa.*

Disciple   *nye-ne.*

Discipline   *drik-lam.*

Discontented, to be   *do-pa mi khang-wa.*

Discourse   *ke-chha.*

Discourse, to   *ke-chha che-pa.*

Discover, to   *thong-wa.*

Discreet (in speech)   *kha tsem-po.*

Discuss, to   *tso-pa gypa-pa.*

Disease   *na-tsha.*

Disgrace   *sham-dren.*

Disguised, to be   *chha-lu mi-chik-po tre-pa.*

Disgusting   *kyuk-tro-po.*

Dish   *der-ma.*

Disheartened   *sem-kyo-po.*

Disk   *khor-lo.*

Dislike, to   *mi-ga-wa.*

Dislocate, to   *tshik-throk-pa.*

Dismantle, to   *shik-pa.*

Dismiss, to   *gong-pho tang-wa;*

Dismount, to   *pap-pa.*

Disobey, to   *kha-la mi-nyem pa.*

Disorder   *go-tro.*

Dispatch, to   *tang-wa.*

Dispensary   *men-khang.*

Disperse, to , v.i.   *trol-wa; kye-pa.*

Disposition   *sem.*

Disputation   *tso-pa.*

Dispute   *lap-shi; tso-pa.*

Disrobe, to   *pi-pa.*

Dissatisfied, to be   *do-pa mi-khang-wa.*

Dissension   *de-tru.*

Dissimilar   *mi-chik-pa.*

Dissimilarity   *khye-par.*

Dissolve, to   *shu-wa.*

Dissuade, to   *sem-gyur-wa.*

Distance   *tha-ring-thung*

Distant   *tha-ring-po.*

Distinct (clear)   *se-po.*

Distinction (difference)   *khye.*

Distinction , to make a   *yen chhe-wa.*

Distinctly (intelligibly)   *dra-tak-po.*

Distinguish, to   *yen-chhe-wa.*

Distinguished (well-known)   *ke-tra chhem-po.*

Distress   *du-nge.*

Distressed, to be   *sem-duk-pa.*

Distribute, to   *go-pa; gop-sha gyap-pa.*

District (tract of country)   *lung-pa; yu.*

Distrust, to   *lo mi khe-pa.*

Disturbance   *gyam-dre.*

Ditch   *chhu-tong.*

Dive, to   *chhu-i-ting-la dzu-dro-wa.*

Divers (various)   *so-so.*

Divest, to (of clothes)   *pi-pa.*

Divide, to   *go-pa; gop-sha. gyap-pa.*

Divorce money   *yuk-je.*

Divorce, to   *kha-trel-wa.*

Dizzy, to be   *go-yu khor-wa.*

Doctor   *am-chhi.*

Doctrine   *chho-lu.*

Document   *dzin.*

Dog   *khyi.*

Dog (for hunting)   *sha-khyi.*

Dominion   *gye-kha.*

Dominoes, to play at   *ba gyap-pa.*

Donkey   *pung-gu.*

Door   *go.*

Door (large outside)   *gye-po.*

Door-frame   *go-rip-shi.*

Door-keeper   *go-ra-pa.*

Dose (of medicine)   *men-thun.*

Dot   *tsha.*

Double   *nyi-dap.*

Doubt   *the-tshom.*

Doubtful   *nye-so.*

Dough   *pa.*

Dove   *tu-tu ku-ku.*

Down   *ma.*

Down hill   *thur.*

Down there   *ma-gi.*

Downwards   *ma.*

Doze, to   *nyi-tso gyap-pa.*

Drag, to   *them-pa.*

Dragon   *druk.*

Drain (on ground)   *yo-po.*

Drain (on roof of house)   *o-chhu.*

Draw lots, to   *mo-gyap-pa.*

Draw out, to (in length)   *ring-tu tang-wa.*

Draw pictures, to   *ri-mo tri-pa.*

Draw up, to (documents)   *tsom-pa.*

Draw, to (pull)   *them-pa.*

29

Drawers (garments) *ko-thung; to-ma.*

Drawers, (in table) *shur-gam.*

Drawers, chest of *gam.*

Dread, to *she-pa.*

Dreadful *she-tra tsha-po.*

Dream *nyi-lam.*

Dream, to *nyi-lam tang-wa.*

Dress, to (clothe) *kyom-pa.*

Dried *kam-po.*

Drill, to (soldiers) *ma-jang che-pa.*

Dringking-water *thung-yo-ki chhu.*

Drink, to *thung-wa.*

Drip, to (of water) *thik-pa gyap-pa.*

Drive, to (Pursue) *te-pa.*

Drop *thik-pa.*

Dropsy, to have *suk-po-la chhu-sak-pa.*

Dross (alloy) *hle.*

Drowned, to be *chhu la shor-wa.*

Drug *men.*

Drum *nga.*

Drum-skin *nga-pa.*

Drum-stick *nga-yo.*

Drunk *rap-si.*

Drunk, to be *ra-si-wa.*

Dry *Kam-po.*

Dry to *kam-pa.*

Dtress *tu-lo.*

Duck *ya-tse.*

Dull (stupid) *kuk-pa; lem pa.*

Dumb *kha-kuk-pa.*

Dung *ri-ma.*

Dupe, to *go-kor tang-wa.*

Durable *tro-chhem-po.*

During *tu-la.*

Dusk *sa-rip.*

Dust *thel-la.*

Dust-storm *the-lung.*

Duty (tax) *sho-thre.*

Dwarf *mi-chhung te-le.*

Dwell, to *de-pa.*

Dweller *do-khen.*

Dwelling, s. *khang-pa; nang; do -sa.*

Dwindle, to (in numbers) *nyung-ru dro-wa*

Dwindle, to (in size) *chhung-ru dro-wa.*

Dye *tsho.*

Dye, to *tsho-gyap-pa.*

Dynasty *gye-gyu.*

Dysentery *thru-ne.*

E

Dyspepsia. *to ma-ju-wa ne.*

Each *re-re.*

Eager *nying-do-po; nying-tro-po.*

Eager to go *dro-nying do-po.*

Eagle *ko-wo.*

Ear *am-cho.*

Ear of corn *nye-ma.*

Ear-hole *am-chho-ki i-khung.*

Early (in morning) *nga-po.*

Earnest, adj. *nying ru chhem-po.*

Earnestly *nying-ru che-ne.*

Earring (man's) *so-chi.*

Earring (of turguoises) *si-yu.*

Earring (woman's) *e-kor.*

Earth *sa.*

Earth work *sap-le.*

Earthen vessel *kho-ma.*

Earthenware *dza-no.*

Earthquake *sa-yom; sa-gu.*

Easily *le-la-po.*

East *shar.*

Easy *le-la-po.*

Eat, to *sa-wa.*

Eating-house *sa-khang.*

Echo *pa-chha.*

Eclipse of the moon *dan-dzin.*

Edge (of knife, etc.) *ngo.*

Edged *no-po.*

Edible, to be *sa-nyem-pa.*

Edict *ka-gya.*

Editor *tsom-pa gyap-khen.*

Educate, to *yi-ge lap-pa; jong-tar tre-pa.*

Efface, to *sup-pa.*

Effect, to (perform) *che-pa.*

Effects (goods) *cha la.*

Effort *lson-dru.*

Egg *go-nga.*

Egg, white of an *kar-trin.*

Eggs, to lay *go-nga tang-wa.*

Eight *gyey.*

Eighteen *chop-gye.*

Eighteenth *chop-gye-pa.*

Eighth *gye-pa.*

Eightieth *gye-chu-pa.*

Eighty *gye-chu.*

Either, conj. *yang-men-na; yang-na.*

Eject, to *tom-pa.*

Elbow *tre-mo.*

Elder brother *cho-cho*

Elder, adj.	*gem-pa.*
Eldest	*gen-sho.*
Elect, to (appoint)	*ko-wa.*
Electric light	*lok-shu.*
Elegant	*dra-chhak-po.*
Element (fire, earth, etc.)	*jung-wa.*
Elephant	*lang-po-chhe; lang-chhen.*
Elevation	*tho-men.*
Eleven	*chuk-chi.*
Eleventh	*chuk-chi-pa.*
Else	*le-min-na.*
Elsewhere	*shem-pa.*
Ember	*men da.*
Emblem	*ta.*
Embrace, to	*khyu-pa.*
Embrassed, to be	*go-thom-pa*
Embroidery	*kying-khap.*
Emerald	*ma-ge.*
Emetic	*kyuk-men.*
Eminence, s.	*gang; tse.*
Eminent, adj.	*ke-tra chhem-po.*
Emperor	*gye-po.*
Emperor's administration	*gye-si.*
Empire	*gyeng-kham.*
Employ, to	*ko-wa.*

Employ, to (servant)	*shak-pa.*
Employment	*le-ka.*
Empty adj,	*tong-pa.*
Enabled, to be	*thup-pa.*
Enamelware	*ku-ku-sha.*
Encamp, to	*gar-gyap-po.*
Encampment	*gar.*
Encircle, to	*kor-wa.*
Enclosure (fence)	*ra-wa.*
Encounter, to (meet)	*thuk-pa.*
Encourage, to	*lo-kho chhe-ru tang-wa.*
End	*tha.*
Endeavour, to	*tson-dru che-pa.*
Endless	*dzo-gyu me-pa.*
Endure, to, v.t.	*so-pa gom-pa.*
Enemy	*dra.*
Energeti	*tsom-po; nying-ru chhem po.*
Engage on hire, to	*la-pa.*
Enhance, to	*phar-wa.*
Enjoin, to	*ka-nang-wa.*
Enjoy, to	*kyi-po. che-pa.*
Enlarge, to	*chhe-ru tang-wa.*
Enmity	*ting-nc.*
Enormous	*chhe-thak-chho.*
Enough, to be	*drik-pa.*

Enquire, to (ask)   *tri-wa.*

Enquire, to (investigate)   *ship-cho che-pa.*

Ensnare, to   *nyi-tsuk-pa.*

Enter, to   *dzu-wa.*

Entertainment (feast)   *drom-po.*

Entice, to   *lu-wa.*

Entire   *tshang-ma tham-che; gang-kha.*

Entirely   *be-te.*

Entomb, to   *so-be lang-wa.*

Entrails   *gyu-ma.*

Entreat, to   *shu-wa.*

Entrust, to   *cho-shok-pa.*

Envelop (tibetan)   *gya-ma.*

Envelope   *yi-koe.*

Envious   *thru-to tsha-po.*

Envoy   *pho-nya.*

Envy, to   *thra-to che-pa.*

Envy, s   *thra-to.*

Epilepsy   *sa-ne.*

Epistle   *yi-ge.*

Equal   *chik-pa; dran-dra.*

Equitable   *dra-trang.*

Erase. to   *sup-pa.*

Erect   *kye-re.*

Erect, to (build)   *tsik-pa.*

Err, to   *nor-wa.*

Error   *nor.*

Eruption (on skin)   *ba-tsha.*

Escape, to   *shor-wa.*

Escort, s.   *ku-sung.*

Especially   *khye par-tu.*

Eternal   *dzo gyu me-pa; tha-me pa.*

Europe   *chhi-ling.*

European, adj.   *chi ling-ki.*

Even, adj.(level)   *nyom-po.*

Even, adv.   *yang.*

Evening   *gong-mo.*

Evenly balanced, to be   *yang-ji me-pa.*

Eveporate, to   *ye-wa.*

Ever (always)   *nam-gyun; tu-gyun : tak-pa re-shi.*

Everlasting   *dzo-gyu me-pa : tha mo-pa.*

Every   *re-re.*

Every kind   *na-tsho.*

Everybody   *mi gang-kha.*

Everyday   *sha-ma re-re.*

Everywhere   *ka sa ka-la.*

Evidence   *gyum-tshen.*

Evident   *nge-par; ngon-ne.*

Evil   *ngen-pa.*

Evil spirit   *dre.*

Exact *thrik-thri.*

Exactly *rang.*

Exactly, so *ta-ka-re.*

Exaggerate, to *ke-chha dro-dok-pa.*

Exalt, to *tho-sa kyel-wa.*

Examination (of student) *gyuk.*

Examine, to (investigate) *ship-cho che-pa.*

Examine, to (student) *gyuk-lem-pa.*

Examined, to be *gyuk-phul-wa.*

Example *pe.*

Example, for *pe-na yin-na; pe-na.*

Excavate, to *ko-wa.*

Excavation *tong.*

Exceed, to *hlak-pa.*

Exceedingly *thak-chho.*

Exceedingly many *mang-thak-chho.*

Excellency, His. *rim-po-chhe.*

Excellent *yak-thak-chho.*

Except *ma-to; mem-pa.*

Excessive *mang-thak-chhu; dzak-lo.*

Excessive appetite *tro-kho chhem-po.*

Exchange *je-po gyap-pa.*

Exclaim, to *ke-lang-wa.*

Excluding (except) *ma-to; mem-pa.*

Excrement (human) *kyak-pa.*

Excuse, s. *khan-dri.*

Excuses, to make *khan-dri she-pa.*

Exercise, literary *yik-gyu*

Exert one's self, to *nying-ru che-pa.*

Exhausted, to be (tired) *thang-chhe-pa.*

Exhaustion *agel.*

Exhibit, to *tem-pa.*

Exhort, to *lap-cha che-pa.*

Exhortation *lap-cha.*

Exist, to *yo-pa.*

Exorcise, to *tam-la tak-pa.*

Expanse *kho-sheng.*

Expect, to (hope for) *re-wa che-pa.*

Expect, to (wait for) *gu-de-pa.*

Expectation *re-wa.*

Expedite, to *tre-wa che pa.*

Expel, to *tom-pa.*

Expense *dro-song.*

Expensive *kong-chhem-po; ku-po.*

Experienced(skilled) *khe-po.*

34

Explain, to   *ngo-tro tre-pa;*
              ton-ta she-pa.

Explain, to (by sign)   *lak-da*
                        che-pa.

Explanation (apology)   *sep-tro.*

Exports   *thon-khung.*

Extensive   *gya-chhem-po.*

External   *chhi-i*

Extinct, to be come   *chhe-pa.*

Extinguish, to   *se-pa.*

Extort, to   *wang-yo che-ne*
             lem-pa.

Extra   *thep-pa.*

Extract, to   *tom-pa.*

Extraction (descent)   *gyu.*

Extraordinary   *yam-tshen po;*
                khye-tsha-po.

Extremity   *tha.*

Exult, to (rejoice)   *ga-wa.*

Exultation   *ga-tshar.*

Eye   *mig.*

Eye lash   *mik-pu.*

Eye-ball   *mik-ri.*

Eye-brow   *mik-si.*

Eye-glass   *mik-sher.*

Eye-glass, hon.   *chen-sher.*

Eye-lid   *mik-pa.*

Eye-lid lower   *mik-pa me.*

Eye-lid upper   *mik pa-ye.*

Eye-shade (of hair)   *mik-ra.*

F

Fable   *drum*

Fabrication (lie)   *ham-pa;*
                    kyak-dzun.

Face   *dhong.*

Facsimile   *dra-shu.*

Fact   *ton-nying.*

Factory   *so-khang.*

Fade, to (wither)   *nyi-pa.*

Fail without (in any event)   *yin-chi*
                    min-chi; ten-den.

Fail, to (miss)   *mi...thup-pa.*

Faint, to   *tren me gye-wa.*

Fair   *dze-po.*

Fair (just)   *thrim-trang-po.*

Fairy   *hla-mo.*

Faith   *te-pa.*

Faithful   *tam-tshi yak-po.*

Fakir   *trup-tho.*

Fall head-over heels, to   *go-*
                          shu lok-pa.

Fall, to   *gye-wa.*

Fall, to (descend)   *pap-yong-*
                     wa (or ro-wa).

Fall, to (descend) hon. *pap-phe-pa.*

Fall, to (from a height) *sak-pa.*

Fallow *sa-long.*

False *ham-pa; kyak-dzun.*

Falsehood *ham-pa; kyak-dzun.*

Falter, to (waver) *the-tshom sa-wa.*

Fame *ke-tra.*

Familiar *lo-ka : nye-po.*

Family *mi-tshang.*

Family (lineage) *ri-gyu.*

Family priest *chho-ne.*

Family, member of *nang-mi.*

Famine *mu-ke.*

Famous (celebrated) *ke-tra chhem-po.*

Fan *lung-khor.*

Fancy (opinion) *sam-pa.*

Fancy (wish) *do-pa.*

Fancy to, (suppose) *sam-pa.*

Fancy, to (like) *ga-wa.*

Fang (of tiger etc.) *chhe-wa.*

Far *tha-ring-po.*

Fare (food) *kha-la; to.*

Farewell ! *ka-le chhip-gyu-nang.*

Farewell (to person going away) *o-na gyu-a.*

Farewell (to person remaining) *o-na do-a.*

Farm *pha-shi.*

Farmer *so-nam che-khen.*

Farming, s.(agriculture) *so-nam.*

Farrier *mik-cha gyang-khen.*

Farther *pha-tsa.*

Fascinate, to *lo-la chhim-pa.*

Fashion (custom) *luk-so.*

Fast (faithful) *tam-tshi yak-po.*

Fast, to *nyung-ne sung-wa.*

Fasten on, to (affix) *drel-wa.*

Fasten, to (with glue etc.) *jar-wa.*

Fasten, to (with rope, etc) *dam-pa.*

Fasting, s. *nyung-ne.*

Fat, adj. *sha-gyak-pa.*

Fat, s. (suet, lard) *tshi-lu.*

Fate *so-de.*

Father *a-pha.*

Father-in-law *pa-la; kyo-po.*

Fatherland *lung-pa.*

Fatigue *ngel.*

Fatiguing *ka-le khak-po.*

Fatiqued, to be *thang-chhe-pa.*

Fault	*kyon.*		Felon	*tsom-pa*
Favour	*trin.*		Felt	*chhing-pa*
Favourite, (official etc.)	*mik-se.*		Female	*mo.*
Fawn	*sha-thru.*		Fence	*ra-wa.*
Fear	*she-tra.*		Fern	*kye-ma.*
Fear, to	*she-pa.*		Ferry	*tru-kha.*
Fearful	*she-tra tsha-po.*		Ferry-boat	*tru.*
Fearless, to be	*she-gyu tsa-ne me-pa.*		Fertile	*lu-chhu dsom-po.*
			Fervent	*nging-ru chhem-po.*
Feast	*drom-po.*		Festival	*tu-chhen.*
Feather (large)	*dro.*		Fever	*tsha-wa.*
Feather (small)	*pu.*		Few	*tok-tsa.*
Features	*sop-ta.*		Fibre	*gyu-pa.*
February	*chin-dha nyee-pa.*		Field	*shing-kha.*
Fee	*ngem-pa; la.*		Fifteen	*cho nga.*
Feeble (infirm)	*kya-re kyo-re; nya-re nyo-re.*		Fifteenth	*cho-nga-pa.*
			Fifth	*nga-pa.*
Feed, to, v.i.	*kha-la sa-wa; to sa-wa.*		Fifty	*ngap-chu.*
			Fight	*gyam-dre.*
Feed, to, v.l.	*to ler-wa.*		Fight, to (make a war)	*ma-gyap-pa.*
Feel cold, to	*khyak-pa.*		Figur (shape)	*sop-ta.*
Feel, to (touch)	*thuk-pa.*		Figure (number)	*ang-ki.*
Feign illness, to	*na-tshu tap-pa.*		File	*chak-sa.*
Feign stupidity, to	*kuk-tshu tap-pa.*		Final	*shuk-sho.*
Feign, to	*kyo-she-pa.*		Find, to	*nye-pa.*
Fellow-labourer	*le-ro.*		Fine(beautiful)	*dze-po.*
Fellow-traveller	*lam-ro.*		Finger	*zu-gu.*

Finger-nail	*sey-mo.*	Flat	*lep-lep.*
Fire	*me.*	Flatten, to	*lep-lep so-wa.*
Fire-place	*thap.*	Flatter, to	*pe-le she-pa.*
Fire-works	*sho-pa.*	Flavour	*tro-wa.*
Firewood	*me-shing.*	Flaw	*kyon.*
First	*tang-po.*	Flay, to	*shu-wa.*
Firstborn	*gem-pa.*	Flea	*jo.*
Fish	*nya.*	Flee, to	*po chhim-pa.*
Fish's fin	*nya--i shok-pa.*	Fleet (quick)	*gyok-po.*
Fish-bone	*nya-ru.*	Flesh	*sha.*
Fish-hook	*cha-kyu; nya-ku.*	Fleshy (fat)	*sha-gyak-pa.*
Fisherman	*nyap dung-nga; nya-sim-khen*	Flexible	*nyem-po.*
Fishing-net	*nya-tol.*	Fling, to	*yuk-pa.*
Fissure	*ser-ka.*	Flint	*me-do.*
Fist	*dzong-go.*	Flip, to	*e-ko shu-wa.*
Fisted, close-	*lak-pa tam-po.*	Float, to	*ding-wa.*
Fit, to (of clothes)	*drik-pa.*	Flock, s.	*khyu.*
Fitting (proper)	*o-po.*	Flog, to	*shu-wa.*
Five	*nga.*	Flood	*chhu ru.*
Fix a time, to	*tu-tsho che-pa.*	Floor, boarded	*pang-lep.*
Fix, to (place)	*shak-pa.*	Flour, barley	*tsam-pa.*
Flag, large	*tar-chhen.*	Flour, wheat	*tro-ship.*
Flagstaff	*tar-shing.*	Flourishing	*yang-chhem-po.*
Flame	*me-che.*	Flout, to (insult)	*me-ra tang-wa.*
Flannel, thin	*ther-ma.*	Flout, to (scoff)	*kya-kya che-ne lap-pa.*
Flannt, to (boast)	*rang-to che-pa.*	Flow out, to	*thom-pa.*

Flow, to   *gyuk-pa.*

Flower   *me-to.*

Fluently   *chhu-gyuk-gyu.*

Fluit (food)   *khu-wa.*

Flute (small)   *ling-pu.*

Fly, s.   *drang-ma.*

Foal.s.   *ti-ki.*

Foam   *ou-wa.*

Fodder (grass and grain)   *tsa-chha.*

Foe   *dra.*

Fog   *muk-pa.*

Fold, to   *tap-tsi gyap-pa.*

Foliage   *lo-ma.*

Folk   *mi.*

Follow, to   *shu-la chhim.*

Fond of, to be   *shen-chha che-pa.*

Fondle, to   *cham po che-pa.*

Fondness   *cham-po*

Food   *kha-laa.*

Food poisoning   *zey-dhoo.*

Fool   *lem-pa; kuk-pa.*

Foolhardy (rash)   *kha-me mik-me.*

Foolish (weak in intellect)   *kuk-pa;*
                                    lem-pa.

Foot   *kang-pa.*

Foot, to go on   *kang-thang-la*
                        dro-wa.

Foot-bridge   *sam-pa*
                    chhung-chhung.

Foot-path   *kang-thang-la dro-sa.*

Foot-print   *kang-je.*

Foot-race   *mi-gyu.*

Foot-soldier   *ma-mi.*

Footstool   *kang-tek.*

For (because)   *ka-re re se-na.*

For (instance)   *pe-sa.*

For (the sake of)   *ton-la.*

Forage (grass)   *tsa.*

Forbear, to   *khok-pa che-pa.*

Forbear, to (of monks)   *so-pa*
                                gom-pa.

Forbid, to   *kak-pa.*

Forbidding (repulsive)   *kyuk-*
                                tro-po.

Force (authority)   *wang.*

Force (strength)   *she.*

Force, to (compel)   *u-tshu*
                            che-pa.

Forcible   *shuk-chhem-po.*

Ford, s.   *rap.*

Forearm   *la-ngar.*

Forecast   *lung-ten.*

Forego, to (renounce)   *pang-wa.*

Foregoing   *ngon-kyi.*

Forehead   *pe-kho.*

39

Foreign   chhi-ling.

Foreign country   phi-ling
                   lung-pa.

Foreigner   chhi-ling-nga.

Foreknowledge   ngon-she.

Forenoon (8 a.m. to 10 a.m.)
                   tsha-ting.

Forerunner   ngen-dru-pa.

Forest   shing-na; nak-sep.

Forete, to, hon.   ngon-khyen
                    khyem-pa.

Foretell, to   ngon-she she-pa.

Foretell, to (in a trance)
                    lung-tem-pa.

Forever   nam-gyun; tu-gyun.

Forget   so-thap.

Forgive, to   gong-pa tang-wa;
               nying-je ta-pa.

Fork   shan-dzin.

Form, s.(shape)   sop-ta.

Form, to (make)   so-wa.

Formally   luk-so nang-shin.

Former   ngon-kyi; tang-po.

Formerly (a short time ago)
                    ngen-la.

Formidable   she-tra tsha-po.

Forsake, to   yuk-shak-pa.

Fort   khar-zong.

Forthwith   lam-sang; lam-kyang.

Fortieth   ship-chu-pa.

Fortification   dzing-ra.

Fortnight   dun-thra nyi; dun-nyi.

Fortress   dzong.

Fortunate   so-de chhem-po;
             so-nam chhem-po.

Fortune, good   so-de; so-nam.

Fortune, bad hon.   ku-so
                     chhung-chhung

Forty   ship-chu.

Foster, to   so-wa.

Foul   tsok-pa.

Found, to (institute)   tsuk-pa.

Foundation of wall   tsik-ten.

Fountain   chhu-mi.

Four   zhi.

Fourteen   chub-zhi.

Fourteenth   chup-shi-pa.

Fourth   shi-pa.

Fowl   cha.

Fox   wa-mo.

Fracture   chhag-dum.

Fragment   chhak-tum.

Fragrance   tri-ma.

Frail (infirm)   kya-re kyo-re;
                  nya-re nyo-re.

Frame, s.   thri.

Frank   trang-po.

Frankincense   *po.*

Frankly   *ma...sang-wa.*

Fraud, to commit   *go-kor-wa.*

Free, to (by ransom)   *lu-wa.*

Free, to become   *thar-wa.*

Free, to v.t.   *thar-ra che-pa tang wa.*

Freedom   *thar-pa.*

Freeze, to   *khyak-pa chhak-pa.*

Frequently   *tshar mang-po.*

Fresco   *ri-mo.*

Fresh   *so-pa.*

Fret, to   *sem thre che-pa; sem-tshap-pa.*

Friction (disagreement)   *thruk-shi.*

Friday   *za pa-sang.*

Fried   *ngo-pa.*

Friend, m.   *trok-po.*

Friendly relationship   *thun-lam.*

Friends, to make   *trok-po gyap-pa.*

Fright (fear)   *she-tra.*

Frighten   *she-tra lang-wa.*

Frighten, to be   *she-pa.*

Frightful   *she-tra tsha-po.*

Frigid   *trang-mo; si-po.*

Fringe (of thrad, etc.)   *kha-tshar; ne-tshar.*

Frivolous   *ton-ne chhung-chhung.*

Frog   *be-pa.*

From   *ne.*

From within   *nang-ne.*

Front of, in (ahead)   *ngen-la.*

Front tooth   *dun-so.*

Frontier   *san-tsham.*

Frost   *khyak-pa.*

Frost-bitten, to be   *kang-ki tshik-pa.*

Froth   *bu-wa.*

Frown, to   *ngo-na du-wa.*

Frozen, to be   *khyak-pa chhak-pa.*

Fruit (of crops)   *dre-pu.*

Fruit of tree (as orange, etc.)   *shing-dre.*

Fruitful (fertile)   *lu-chhu dzom-po.*

Fruitless, to be (useless)   *phen mi thok-pa.*

Fry, to   *ngo-pa.*

Frying pan   *tshay-lang.*

Frying-pan   *tshe-lang*

Fuel   *me-shing.*

Fulfil, to   *drup-pa.*

Fulfilled, to be   *tshar-wa.*

Full   **kang.**

Fun   **te-mo.**

Function (work)   *le-ka.*

Functionary   *pom-po.*

Fundament   *kup.*

Fungus   *sha-mo.*

Funny   *ge-mo tro-po.*

Fur   *pu.*

Fur-coat   *pak-tsha.*

Furnace   *thap.*

Furnish, to (supply)   *drup-pa.*

Furniture   *cha-la.*

Furrow   *ro.*

Further (in distance)   *pha-tsa.*

Fuse (for gun)   *bi-di.*

Futile, to be (useless)   *phen mi thok-pa.*

Future   *shu-la.*

G

Gaiety   *ga-tshor.*

Gain (profit)   *khep-sang.*

Gain victory, to   *gye-wa.*

Gain, to (obtain)   *jor-wa; thop-pa.*

Gainsay, to (deny)   *gyam-ge lap-pa.*

Gainsay, to (dispute)   *tso-pa gyap-pa.*

Gait   *dro-tang.*

Gale   *hlak-pa tsha-po.*

Gall (malignant feeling)   *no-sem.*

Gall-bladder   *thri-pa.*

Gallant, adj.   *nying-chhem-po.*

Gallant, hon.   *thu-nying chhem-po.*

Gallop, to   *sham-pe tang-wa.*

Gamble, to   *sho-gyap-pa.*

Gambler   *sho-pa.*

Game (play)   *tse-mo.*

Game (wild animals)   *ri-ta.*

Gander   *ang-pa.*

Gang   *tsho.*

Gaol   *tson-khang.*

Gaoler   *tson-suna-nga.*

Gap   *se-ka.*

Gape, to (of wounds)   *kha-sha de-pa.*

Garb   *tu-lo.*

Garden   *dum-ra.*

Gardener   *ling-sung-nga.*

Gargle, to   *kha-she-she tang wa.*

Garland   *me-to thrang-nga.*

Garlic   *gok-pa.*

Garment   *tu-lo.*

Garnish, to (adorn)   *gyen-cha tak-pa.*

Garrison   *ma-pa.*

Garter (for Tibetan boots)   *hlam-dro.*

Gas   *tu-we lang-pa.*

Gas, poisonous   *tuk-lang*

Gate (large)   *gye-po.*

Gate (small)   *chhi-go.*

Gather, to (assemble) v.i.   *tsok-pa; dzom-pa.*

Gather, to (collect) v.t.   *du-pa.*

Gather, to (pick up)   *druk-pa.*

Gather, to (pluck off tree)   *tok-pa.*

Gaunt   *sha kam-po.*

Gay, to be   *ga-wa; kyi-po che-ne do-pa.*

Gelding   *pho-ta.*

Gem   *nor-pu.*

Gender   *pho-mo.*

Genealogy (of laymen)   *ri-gyu; mi-gyu.*

Generally   *phe-chher.*

Generate, to   *kye-pa.*

Generation   *mi-gyu.*

Generosity   *trin.*

Generous   *lak-pa shok-po.*

Genius   *rik-pa.*

Gentian   *tik-ta.*

Gentile   *chhi-pa.*

Gentle   *jam-po.*

Gentleman   *ku-tra.*

Gently (slowly)   *ka-le.*

Genuine   *ngo-tho; ngo-ne.*

Geography   *dzam-ling gye-she.*

Germinate, to   *kye-wa.*

Gesture   *dap.*

Gesture of foot   *kang dap.*

Gesture of hand   *lak-dap.*

Get by heart, to   *lo-la sim-pa.*

Get through, to   *thar-wa.*

Get up, to v.i.   *lang-wa.*

Get well, to   *trak-pa.*

Get, to   *jor-wa; thop-pa.*

Ghastly (horrible)   *she-tra tsha-po.*

Ghost   *dong-dre; dre.*

Giant   *mi-chhem-po.*

Gibberish   *ton-ta me-pe ke-chha.*

Gibe, to   *kya-kya che-ne lap-pa.*

Giddy, to be   *go-yu khor-wa; si-yom-yom che-pa.*

Gift (alms to poor)   *jim-pa.*

Gigantic   *chhe-thak-chho.*

Giggle, to   *kha tshe-tshe che-pa.*

Gild, to (images etc.)   *tsha-ser tang-wa.*

Gilding   *tsha-ser.*

Gilt, s.   *tsha-ser.*

Gimlet   *sor.*

Ginger   *ga-mu.*

Girdle   *ke-ra.*

Girl   *pu mo.*

Girth (of saddle)   *lo.*

Gist (of letter, etc.)   *ton-nying.*

Give over, to (deliver)   *tre-pa.*

Give up, to   *pang-wa.*

Give, to   *ter-wa.*

Give, to (to superior)   *phu-wa.*

Gize, to   *ta-wa.*

Glacier   *khya-rum.*

Glad, to be   *ga-wa.*

Gladness   *ga-tshor.*

Glaring   *o-chhem-chhem.*

Glass   *shay.*

Gleam, to   *o gyap-pa.*

Glee   *ga-tshor.*

Gleeful, to be   *ga-wa.*

Glimmer, to   *o gyap-pa.*

Glisten, to   *o gyap-pa.*

Glistening, adj.   *o chhem-po.*

Glitter, to   *o gyap-pa.*

Globe   *ri-ri.*

Globular   *ri-ri.*

Glomy, to be (low-spirited)   *sem kyo-nang che-pa.*

Gloom   *mi-na.*

Glorious (in appearance)   *si-ji chhem-po.*

Glory (splendour)   *si-ji.*

Glossary   *ming-dzo.*

Glossy (of silk)   *kon-yak-po.*

Glue   *ping.*

Gluttonous   *tro-chhem-po.*

Gnash teeth, to   *so-dar-wa.*

Gnat   *sin-drang.*

Gnaw to   *mur-wa.*

Go after, to   *shu-la chhim-pa.*

Go between   *par-mi.*

Go down, to (hill, etc.)   *thur-la pap-pa.*

Go out, to   *thom-pa.*

Go round, to   *khor-wa.*

Go up, to   *dzak-pa.*

Go, to   *dro-wa.*

Goat   *ra.*

Goat, he   *ra-pho.*

44

Goat, she   *ra-mo.*

Goblin   *dong-dre; dre.*

God   *kun-chho.*

God, a   *hla.*

Goddess, a   *hla-mo.*

Godless   *chho sem me-pa.*

Godown   *to-khang.*

Goggles   *mik-she.*

Goitre   *ba-a.*

Gold   *ser.*

Golden   *ser-dhog.*

Goldsmith   *ser-so-wa.*

Gong   *kha-nga.*

Gonorrhoea   *trang-shi.*

Good for, to be   *phen thok-pa.*

Good, adj.   *yak-po.*

Good, s. (advantage)   *phen.*

Good-bye ! (to person remaining)   *o-na do-a.*

Good-bye (to person going)   *o-na gyu-a.*

Good-tempered   *gyu-ma ring-po.*

Goodbye   *ga-le pheb.*

Goodluck   *tashi delek.*

Goods   *cha-la.*

Goose   *ngang-pa.*

Gorge   *rong.*

Gorgeous (of person)   *ngam-si chhem-po.*

Gossamer   *dom-tha.*

Gossip, to   *lap-lap dung-wa; khap-le she-pa.*

Gout   *bam.*

Govern a country, to   *gyo-si nang-wa.*

Govern, to   *wang-che-pa.*

Government   *shung : shung tho.*

Government revenue   *shung gi bap.*

Governor   *ka lon.*

Gown   *chhu-pa.*

Gown, hon.   *nam-sa.*

Grace (favour)   *ka-trin; thuk-je.*

Graceful   *dze-po.*

Gracious   *trin-chhem-po.*

Grade (rank)   *ko-ṣa; ko-ne; rim-pa.*

Gradually   *ka-le ka-le.*

Grain (for animals)   *chha.*

Grain (for human beings)   *dru.*

Grain, parched   *yo.*

Grammar (orthography)   *tak-yi.*

Granary   *dru-kang-juk; dru-khang.*

Grand   *chhem-po.*

Grand daughter	*pu-i pu-mo; pu-mo pu-mo.*
Grand father	*po-o.*
Grand mother	*mo-o.*
Grandson (son's son)	*pu-i-pu.*
Grant, to	*ter-wa.*
Grape (fruit)	*gun-drum.*
Grasp, to (understand)	*ha-ko-wa.*
Grasp, to	*sim-pa.*
Grasping (avaricious)	*ham-pa chhem-po.*
Grass	*tsa.*
Grateful	*ka-trin chhem-po.*
Grateful, to be	*trin trem-pa.*
Gratification (Pleasure)	*ga-tshor.*
Gratified, to be	*ga-wa.*
Grating (for windows)	*thra-ma.*
Gratitude	*ka trin nying-chang.*
Gratuity (tip)	*chhang-rin.*
Grave, s.	*tur-khung.*
Gravity (importance)	*nen-kha.*
Gravy	*sha-khu.*
Gray	*ngop-kya.*
Graze, to (eat grass)	*tsa sa-wa.*
Grease	*tshi-lu.*
Greasy	*shak-tsi chhem-po.*
Great	*chhem-po.*
Greed	*ham-pa.*
Greedy (avaricious)	*do-pa chhem-po.*
Green	*jang-khu.*
Green (of grass)	*ngom pa.*
Greet, to (by raising the hands)	*dam jel che pa.*
Grey	*thal-dhog.*
Grief (in serious matters)	*du nge; sem thre.*
Grim	*she-ta tsha-po.*
Grind, to (Corn)	*tok-pa.*
Grind, to (steel the teeth)	*dar-wa.*
Grindstone	*dar-da.*
Grip, to	*sim-pa.*
Groan, to	*ke-shor-wa.*
Grog-seller	*chhang-ma.*
Grog-shop	*chhang-khang.*
Groom	*chhip-pon.*
Grotto	*trak-phu.*
Ground	*sa.*
Ground-rent	*sap-la.*
Group	*tsho.*
Grouse, sand	*kang-ka-ling.*
Grove, pleasure	*ling-ka.*
Grow dark, to	*sa-rip-pa.*
Grow old, to	*ge-ru ge-ru dro-wa.*
Grow, to	*chhe-ru chhe-ru dro-wa.*

46

Gruel   *pa thu.*

Gruff (surly)   *kyong-po.*

Grunt, to   *ke-gyap-pa.*

Guarantee   *khe-khya.*

Guarantee, to   *khe-khya che-pa.*

Guarantor   *khe-khya che-khen.*

Guard, s.   *sung-khen.*

Guard, to (a place)   *sung-wa.*

Guard, to (take care of goods)
                    nyar-wa.

Guardian   *gon-don che-khen.*

Guess, s.   *tsho.*

Guest   *drom-po.*

Guest house   *don-khang.*

Guide, s.   *lam gyu che-khen;*
             lam-kha ten-khen

Guide, to   *lam-gyu che-pa;*
             lam-kha tem-pa.

Guile   *yo-gyu.*

Guileful   *yo-gyu tsha-po.*

Guilt   *kyon; nye-pa.*

Guiltless   *nye-pa me-pa.*

Guilty   *kyon-chhem-po;*
          nye-pa chhem po.

Guinea-pig   *ab-ra.*

Guitar   *dram-nyen.*

Gull, to   *go-kor tang-wa.*

Gullet   *mik-pa.*

Gully   *nrang-ga.*

Gum   *jar-tsi.*

Gum   *jar-tsi.*

Gum (of teeth)   *so-nying.*

Gums   *so-sha.*

Gun   *men-da.*

Gun, stock of   *gum-shing.*

Gun, hammer of   *kam-pa.*

Gun, ramrod of   *sim-bi.*

Gun-barrel   *cha-hrang.*

Gun-fuse   *li-di.*

Gun-powder   *dze.*

Gun-rest (of Tibetan fashion)
                    men-de ru.

Guts   *gyu-ma.*

Gutter (on ground)   *yo-po.*

H

Habit   *luk-so.*

Habitation   *khang-pa; nang;*
              do-sa.

Habitually   *tak-pa; nam-gyun.*

Haemorrhoids (piles)   *trang-thor.*

Haft   *yu-wa.*

Hag   *ma-gen.*

Hail, s.   *se-ra.*

Hail, to (ailstorm)   *se-ra tang-wa.*

Hair (of animals, human)   *pu.*

Hair (on human head)   *tra.*

Hair (on body)   *pu.*

Hair (on head)   *ta.*

Hair, a single   *tra-kang chi.*

Hair, to wash the   *tra thru-pa.*

Hair-brush   *phak-se.*

Hairs, two   *tra-kang-nyi.*

Half   *chhe-ka.*

Hall of assembly   *tshom-chhen.*

Halo   *O-kor.*

Halt, to   *shak-sa do-pa.*

Halter   *thong-go.*

Halting-place (for the day)
　　　　　　　shak-sa.

Hammer   *tho-wa.*

Hamper, to (hinder)   *kak-pa.*

Hamper, s.   *le ko.*

Hamper, to (hinder) hon.   *kak-ka
　　　　　　　nang-wa.*

Hand   *lag-pa.*

Handcuff, to   *lak-cha gyap-pa.*

Handcuffs   *lak-cha.*

Handful, a   *bar-ra kang.*

Handicraft   *le-ka.*

Handkerchief   *nap-chhi.*

Handkerchief (compliment)
　　　　　　　kha-ta.

Handle, to   *chhang-wa.*

Handle, curved (of kettle, &c.)
　　　　　　　lung.

Handle, straight (of knife, &c.)
　　　　　　　yu-wa.

Handmaid   *yo-mo.*

Handsome   *tshar-po : dze-po.*

Handwriting   *yi-ge.*

Hang, to (a man)   *k-la thak-pa
　　　　　　　dam-ne se-pa.*

Hang, to v.i.   *kel-wa.*

Hanker after to   *trem-pa.*

Happen, to   *chung-wa.*

Happiness   *ga-tshor.*

Happy (comfortable)   *kyi-po.*

Happy, to be   *ga-wa.*

Harm, to (by witchcraft, &c.) *no-pa.*

Harmony, to be in   *thum-pa.*

Harp   *dram-nyen.*

Harsh   *kyong-po.*

Hart   *sha a.*

Harvest   *ton-tho.*

Haste   *tre-wa.*

Hasten, to   *gyok-po che-pa.*

Hastily   *lam-sang.*

Hasty (quick)   *gyok-po.*

Hasty (rash)   *kha-me mik-me.*

Hat   *sha-mo.*

Hat   *zha-mo.*

Hat, hon.   *u-sha.*

Hatchet   *ta-ri; ta-tru.*

Hate, to   *dang po che-pa.*

Hateful   *kyuk-tro-po.*

Haughtiness   *nyam; dza-kho.*

Haughty   *nyam-chhem-po; dza-kho chhem-po.*

Haul, to   *them-pa.*

Haunt, s.   *tshang.*

Have, I   *nga-la yo.*

Have, to   *yo-pa.*

Haversack   *to-phe.*

Hawk   *thra.*

Hay   *sem-pa; tsa-kam-po.*

Hay-fork   *khep-ra.*

Hay-sickle   *sor-ra.*

Hazard   *nyen-kha.*

Hazardous   *nyen-kha chhem-po.*

Haze   *muk-pa.*

He   *kho; kho-rang.*

Head   *go.*

Head (leader)   *go-pa.*

Head shaved (as a monk)   *go-ri.*

Headache   *go-ney.*

Headman   *go-che.*

Headstrong   *kyong-po.*

Heal, to   *trak-ka so-wa.*

Heal, to (patient of good position)   *ku-tang-nga so-wa nang-wa.*

Healed, to be   *trak-pa.*

Health   *suk-po; kham.*

Healthy   *suk-po de-po.*

Heap, s.   *pung.*

Hear, to   *ko-wa; am-chho ko-wa.*

Hearken, to   *nyem-pa.*

Hearsay (report)   *ke-chha; tam.*

Heart   *nying.*

Heart, to learn by   *lo-la sim-pa.*

Hearth   *thap.*

Heartily   *nying-ru che-ne.*

Heat   *tshe-pa.*

Heathen   *chhi pa.*

Heaven (sky)   *nam; nam-kha.*

Heavy   *ji-po.*

Hedge   *ra-a.*

Hedgehog   *sik-mo.*

Heed, to   *nyem-pa.*

Heel   *ting-pa.*

Heifer   *pe-pe.*

Height   *tho-tshey.*

Heir   *nor-kyi dak-po.*

Heiress   *nor-kyi dak-po.*

Hell   *nyel-la.*

Hello *o-loy.*

Helmet *mo.*

Help *ro.*

Help, to *ro che-pa.*

Helper *ro-che-khen.*

Helpful, to be (useful)
                        phen-thok-pa.

Helpless *ro.......me pa.*

Hem, to *ne ne tshem-pa.*

Hem, s. *ne; ne-mo.*

Hemp *so-ma ra-tsa.*

Hen *cha-mo.*

Hence (from this place) *di-ne.*

Henceforth *ta-ne chhin-chhe.*

Her *mo.*

Herd *khyu.*

Herdsman *dzi-o.*

Herdsman of sheep *luk-dzi.*

Here *de.*

Hereafter *ta-ne chhin-chhe.*

Heresy *chho-lo.*

Heresy, to commit *chho-lo
                        che-pa.*

Herewith *di-tang nyam-tu.*

Heritage *nor-ke.*

Hermit *gom-chhen.*

Hermitage *en-ne.*

Hero *pa-o.*

Heroine *pa-mo.*

Hers *mo.*

Herself *kho-rang.*

Hesitate, to *the-tshom sa-wa.*

Hesitation *the-tshom.*

Hiccough, to *i-ka gyap-pa.*

Hidden (concealed) *be-pa.*

Hideous *she-tra tsha-po.*

Hierarchy *chho-si.*

High (of things, rank of persons)
                        tho-po.

Highway *gya-lam.*

Hill *ri.*

Hilt *yu-wa.*

Him *kho-la.*

Hind-foot *kang-pa.*

Hinder, to *kak-pa.*

Hindrance *kak-chha.*

Hinge (of Tibetan make) *ting-pa.*

Hip *chee-go.*

Hire (wages) *la; pho.*

Hire, to *le-pa.*

Hired workman *mi-la; la-pa.*

His *kho.*

History *gyay-rab.*

Hit at, to (with a stick etc.)
                        shu-wa.

Hit, to *khe-pa; phok-pa.*

Hit, a   *cha.*

Hither   *tshur; di-ru.*

Hitherto   *ta-thu par-tu.*

Hive (of bees)   *lrang-tshang.*

Hoar-frost   *pa-mo.*

Hoard   *kang-juk.*

Hoarse, to be   *ke dzer-wa.*

Hobbling (lame)   *kang-kyo.*

Hobgoblin   *dong-dre; dre.*

Hoe   *jo.*

Hoe, to   *ko-wa.*

Hog   *phak-pa.*

Hoist, to   *yar-chhar-wa.*

Hold up, to   *tem-pa.*

Hold, to (catch hold of)   *sim-pa.*

Hole (made by human being or animal   *khung.*

Hole, peep   *so-khung.*

Holiday   *gong-pa.*

Hollo ! interj.   *we.*

Hollow, adj.   *khok-tong.*

Hollow, s. (in the ground)   *kong-tong.*

Hollyhock   *ha-lo me-to.*

Holy   *tam-pa chhon-den.*

Homage, to do   *chha-tshe-wa.*

Home   *nang; khang-pa.*

Home, at   *nang-la.*

Home-sick, to be   *lung-pa trem-pa.*

Honest   *trang-po.*

Honey   *drang-tsi.*

Honour (respect)   *nyen-kur.*

Hood (as scarf wound round the face   *kha-tri.*

Hoof   *mik-pa.*

Hook   *kuk.*

Hook, fish   *nya-kuk.*

Hook, iron   *cha-kyu.*

Hookah   *hor-kha.*

Hookah, bowl of   *chi-lim.*

Hoop   *shen.*

Hoopoe   *pu-pu khu-shu.*

Hope   *re-wa.*

Hope, to   *re-wa che-pa.*

Hopeless, to be   *re-wa me-pa*

Horizon   *thong-we khor.*

Horn   *ra-cho.*

Hornet   *drang-ma.*

Hornless   *a-yu.*

Horoscope   *kye-ka tak-pa.*

Horoscope, hon.   *thrung-ka tak-pa.*

Horrible   *she-tra tsha-po.*

Horrid   *she-tra tsha-po.*

Horrifying   *she-tra tsha-po.*

Horror   she-tra.

Horse   ta.

Horse, saddle   shon-ta.

Horse, chinese   sing-ta.

Horse, pack   khe-ta.

Horse-dung   te-bang.

Horse-shoe   mik-cha.

Horse-whip   te-cha.

Horseman   ta-pa.

Horsemen, body of   tap-ra.

Hospitable   lak-pa shok-po.

Hospital   men-khang.

Hospital   men-khang.

Host (army)   ma.

Hostess   ne-mo.

Hot   tsha-po.

Hot (of weather)   tshe-pa
tsha-po.

Hot water   chhu tsha-po.

Hot, to be (of body)   tshe-pa
tshik-pa.

Hot-tempered   lung lang-po.

Hotel   don-khang; za-khang.

Hotel-charges   ne-la.

Hotel-keeper   ne-po.

Hound   khyi.

Hour   chhu-tsho.

House   nang; khang-pa.

House, caretaken of
khang-sung-nga.

House-agent   khang-nyer.

House-hold   nang-mi.

House-owner   khang-dak.

House-rent   khang-la.

Housewife   ne-mo.

Hovel   nang-chhung;
khang-chhung.

How   kan-dre.

How much   ka-tsho.

Howbeit   ka-re yin-ne.

However   yin-ne; yin-kyang;
yin-na-yang.

Howl, to (of dogs)   duk-ke
gyap-pa.

Hug, to   khyu-pa.

Huge   chhe-thak-chho.

Hullo ! (expression of surprise)
a-tsi.

Human   mi-i.

Humble   sem-chhung-chhung.

Humid   lom-pa.

Humorous   ge-mo tro-po.

Hunch-back   to-gur.

Hundred   gya-tham-pa.

Hundredth   gya-tham-pa.

Hunger   tok-pa.

Hungry, to be   tro kho tok-pa.

Hunt, to   *khyi-ra gyap-pa.*

Hunter   *khyi-ra-wa.*

Hurricane   *hlak-pa tsha-po.*

Hurry, in a great   *tre-wa tsha-po che-ne.*

Hurry, to   *gyok-po che-pa.*

Hurt (physical)   *ma.*

Hurt, to be   *kyon-che-pa.*

Hurt, to (impair)   *kyon-che-pa.*

Husband   *khyo-ka.*

Husband and wife   *sa-tshang.*

Husbandman   *so-nam che-khen.*

Husbandry (agriculture)   *so-nam.*

Husk (of grain)   *pak-pa.*

Hut   *nang-chhung; khang-chhung.*

Hydrophobia   *khyim-nyon.*

Hymn   *gur-ma.*

I

I   *nga.*

Ice   *khvak-pa.*

Icy, to be   *khyak-pa yo-pa.*

Idea (opinion)   *sam pa.*

Idea (purport)   *ton.*

Identical   *chik-pa.*

Identify, to   *ngo-thro tre-pa.*

Idiom   *ke-lu.*

Idiot   *kuk-pa; lem-pa.*

Idiotic (stupid)   *kuk-pa; lem-pa.*

Idle   *gyu-ma ring po; le-lo chhem-po.*

Idol   *kun-dra.*

If   *ke-si...na.*

Ignite, to   *bar-wa.*

Ignoble   *kye-sa ma-po.*

Ignominious   *ngo-tsha-po.*

Ignominy   *ngo-tsha.*

Ignoramus   *kuk-pa.*

Ignorant   *yon-ten me-pa.*

Ill, to be   *na-wa.*

Ill-fated   *so-de me-pa; so-de chhung-chhung.*

Ill-feeling, to cherish   *sem-la ngem-pa che-ne shak-pa.*

Ill-luck   *so-de me-pa.*

Ill-natured   *sem-ngem-pa.*

Ill-will   *nying-ne.*

Illegal   *thrim-me.*

Illegitimate   *thrim-me.*

Illicit   *thrim-me.*

Illimitable   *tsho-me-pa.*

Illiterate, to be   *yon-ten me-pa.*

Illness   *na-tsha.*

Illuminate, to   *O-gyap-pa.*

Illusion (optical)   *mik-thru.*

Illusive   *mik-thru chhem-po.*

Illustrate, to   *pe-jar-ne she-pa.*

Illustration   *pe.*

Illustrious   *ke-tra chhem-po.*

Image (idol)   *kun-dra.*

Imagination   *mik-pa.*

Imagine, to (think)   *sam-pa.*

Imbecile   *kuk-pa; lem-pa.*

Imbrue, to (soak)   *bang-wa.*

Imitate, to   *mik-dren che-pa.*

Immaculate, to be   *kyon me pa.*

Immaterial (without substance)
   su-me.

Immeasurable (very great)   *chhe thak chho.*

Immediately   *lam-sang.*

Immense   *gya-chhem-po; chhe thak-chho.*

Immoderate, to be   *tsho-me-pa.*

Immodest, to be   *ngo-tsha me-pa.*

Immoral   *che-tang ngem-po.*

Immortal, to be
   shi-gyu....me-pa.

Immovable   *yo-gyu me-pa.*

Impair, to   *kyon-che-pa.*

Impale, to   *shing-la ke-ne se-pa.*

Impart, to   *ter-wa.*

Impartial   *nye-ring me-pa.*

Impartial (of judges)   *thrim trang-po.*

Impassable to be   *mi...thar-wa.*

Impassive   *trem pa gyel-wa.*

Impede, to   *kak-pa.*

Impediment   *kak-chha.*

Imperceptible, to be
   thong-gyu me-pa.

Imperfect   *mi tak-pa.*

Imperfection (defect)   *kyon.*

Imperial   *gye-po.*

Imperishable, to be   *chha-gyu me-pa.*

Impertinent   *jing-pa bom-po; kyong-po.*

Impetuous   *ru-ngar-po.*

Impious   *chho sem me-pa.*

Implements   *lak-chha.*

Implore, to   *shu-wa.*

Impolite   *kyong-po.*

Import (meaning)   *ton-ta.*

Importance   *nen kha.*

Important   *nen-kha chhem-po, ke-chhem-po.*

Impose on, to (deceive)
   go-kor-wa.

Impose, to (lay on)   *ku-wa.*

Imposition (deceit) *go-kor.*

Impossible *mi-thup-pa.*

Impost (general) *thre; bap.*

Imposture *go-kor.*

Impotent, to be *top-chhak-pa.*

Impracticable, to be *che..mi thup-pa.*

Imprecate, to *mo-mo gyap-pa.*

Impression thumb *dzuk-the.*

Imprison, to *tson-la chuk-pa.*

Improper *mi-chhok-pa.*

Improve, to *so-kyor che-pa.*

Impudent *jing-pa bom-po; kyong-po.*

Impure *kyuk-tro-po.*

Impurity *trip.*

Impute, wrongly, to *ya-la shak-pa.*

In (inside) *nang-la.*

Inaccessible *tsem-po.*

Inaccurate, to be *mi tak-pa.*

Inadequate, to be *mi drik-pa.*

Inattentive, to be *sem-yang-ne de-pa.*

Inauspicious day *yang-sa.*

Incalculable *trang-me.*

Incantation *nga.*

Incapable *mi...thup-pa.*

Incarcerate, to *tson-la chuk-pa.*

Incarnate lama *tul-ku.*

Incarnate, to be *trul-wa.*

Incarnation (of a deity) *trul-ku.*

Incautious *nang-ta me-pa.*

Incense, s. *po.*

Incense, to *khong-thro lang-wa.*

Incessant *gyun-chhe-gyu me-pa.*

Incessantly *nam-gyun; tu-gyun.*

Inch (breadth of a finger) *sor.*

Inclination *do-pa.*

Incline, to (lean against) *bo-nye gyap-pa.*

Inclined, to be *do-pa yo-pa.*

Inclosure *ra-wa.*

Include, to *dom-pa.*

Income *thop-thang.*

Incompetent, to be *o-po me-pa.*

Incomplete, to be *mi tshang-wa.*

Inconstant, to be *tem-po me-pa.*

Incorporeal *suk-po me-pa.*

Incorrect *ma-tak-pa.*

Increase (in size)   *chhe-ru*
                      chhe-ru dro-wa.

Increase, to (in numbers)
                      phe-wa.

Indeed   *ten-ten; ngo-tho.*

Indefatigable   *nying-ru*
                chhem-po.

Indefinite   *tem-po me-pa.*

Indented   *kyong-kyong.*

Independent   *rang-go thom-pa.*

Indestructible   *chha-gyu*
                  me-pa.

Index   *tho.*

India   *gya-kar.*

India (plains of)   *gya-thang.*

Indian   *gya-kar-kyi.*

Indicate, to   *mi-tom-pa.*

Indifferent, to be   *nang-ta*
                      mi-che-pa.

Indige   *ram.*

Indigent   *kyo-po.*

Indigestion   *to ma ju-we ne.*

Indignant, to be   *khong-thro sa-wa;*
                    tshik-pa sa-wa.

Indignation   *tshik-pa;*
               khong-thro.

Indisposed, to be (unwell)   *de-po*
  me-pa; suk-po thang-po me-pa

Indisposition (illness)   *na-tsha.*

Indistinct   *se-po me-pa.*

Indolent   *gyu-ma ring-po; le-lo*
            chhem-po.

Indra   *hlai-wang-po gya-jin.*

Induce, to   *u-tshu che-pa.*

Industrious   *nying-ru*
               hhem-po.

Industry   *nying-ru.*

Ineffaceable, to be   *sup...mi*
                       thup-pa.

Inefficient, to be   *o-po...me-pa.*

Inequitable, to be (unjust)
                      trang-po...me-pa.

Inert, to be   *hur-po me-pa.*

Inexhaustible   *dzo-gyu me-pa.*

Inexorable   *ma-wa len-chi.*

Inexpensive   *khe-po;*
               kong-chhung-chhung.

Infallible, to be.   *mi-nor-wa.*

Infamy   *ming ngen.*

Infant   *pu-gu chhung-chhung.*

Infant (of a few weeks only)
                      man-ja.

Infantry   *mak-pung.*

Infelicitous (unfortunate)   *su-de*
  me-pa : so-de chhung chhung.

Inferior (of things)   *duk-po.*

Infertile   *tsa-chhu*
             dzom-po...me-pa.

Infirm   *she me-pa.*

Inflame, to (with anger)
    khong-thro lang-wa.

Inflamed, to be (of hands &c.)
    tshik-pa.

Inflammation   *tsha-wa.*

Inflate, to   *kam-phu gyang-wa.*

Inflexible (stubborn)   *kyong-po.*

Influence   *wang.*

Influential   *wang-chhem-po.*

Inform, to   *len-tro-pa.*

Information (news)   *ne-tshul; sang gyu.*

Informer   *len-tre-khen.*

Ingemous   *chu-khe-po.*

Inhabit, to   *de-pa.*

Inhale, to   *u-them-pa.*

Inherit, to   *ke-la thop-pa.*

Inheritance   *thop-ke.*

Inhibit, to (forbid)   *kak-pa.*

Inhuman, to be   *nying-je me-pa.*

Inimical, to be   *dra-che-pa.*

Iniquious   *ngem-po.*

Inject, to   *chuk-pa.*

Injunction   *ka.*

Injure, to(by witchcraft, etc.)
    no-pa che-pa.

Injured, to be   *kyon-che-pa.*

Injury   *no-pa.*

Injustice, to do   *thrim-me che-pa.*

Ink   *nag-tsha.*

Ink red   *tshe.*

Ink-pot   *nak-pum.*

Inlet (bay)   *chhu-hla.*

Inmate, (fellow lodger)
    to-tshang; thap-ro.

Inn   *ne-tshang.*

Inn-keeper   *ne po.*

Inner   *nang-ki.*

Innocent   *nye-pa me-pa.*

Innumerable   *trang me.*

Inoculate, to (for smallpox)
    hlan-drum tsuk-pa.

Inordinate, to be   *tsho me-pa.*

Inquire, to (into a matter)   *tse cho-pa.*

Inquire, to   *tri-wa.*

Inquire, to (investigate)
    ka-ship nang-wa

Inquire, to(investigate)
    ship-cho che-pa.

Inquiry (investigation)   *ship-cho.*

Insane   *nyom-pa.*

Inscription   *do-ko.*

Insect   *bu.*

Insensible, to become   *trem-pa thor-wa.*

Inseparable, to be   *tre...mi-thup-pa.*

Insert, to   *tsuk-pa.*

Inside, prep.   *nang-la.*

Insignificant (of matters)   *ton ta chhung-chhung.*

Insist, to   *u-tshu che-pa.*

Insoluble   *shu...mi thup-pa.*

Inspect, to   *ta-wa.*

Installation (of a ruler)   *thrin-don.*

Instance   *pe.*

Instance, for   *pe-na.*

Instant, in an (presently)   *hrip-tsa-chi-la.*

Instantaneously   *lam-sang; lam-kyang.*

Instantly   *lam-sang; lam-kyang.*

Instead of   *tshap-la.*

Instigate, to   *ngen-pa lap-pa.*

Institute, to   *tsuk-pa.*

Instruct, to   *lap-pa.*

Instructor   *ge-gen; lo-pon.*

Instrument   *lak-chha.*

Insufficient   *mi...dang wa.*

Insult, s.   *me-ra.*

Insult, to   *me-ra tang-wa.*

Insurrection   *de-thruk.*

Intellect   *lo-tro.*

Intellectual   *lo-tro chhem-po.*

Intelligence (news)   *ne-tshul; sang-gyu.*

Intelligent   *rik-pa yak-po.*

Intemperate, to be   *tsho-me-pa.*

Intend, to (purpose)   *sem-la sam-pa.*

Intent, s.   *ton-ta.*

Intention   *ton-ta.*

Inter, to (bury)   *sa-la be-pa.*

Intercede, to   *par-mi che-pa.*

Intercede, to hon.   *Par-mi nang-wa.*

Intercourse, to have (conversation)   *ke-chha che-pa.*

Interdict, to (forbid)   *kak-pa.*

Interest, (on loan)   *kye.*

Interior, s.(of a building)   *nang.*

Internal   *nang-ki.*

Interpose, to (intercede)   *par-mi che-pa.*

Interpreter   *lo-tsa-wa.*

Interrogate, to   *tri-wa.*

Interrupt, to   *kak-pa.*

Interruption   *kak-chha.*

Interstice   *ser-ka.*

Intestines   *gyu-ma.*

Intidel   *chhi-pa.*

Intimate, adj   *ga-po nye-po.*

Intimidate, to   *she-tra lang-wa.*

Into   *nang-la.*

Intolerable (pain)   *gong mi thup-pa.*

Intonation   *dang.*

Intoxicated   *ra-si.*

Intrepid   *nying-chhem-po.*

Intricate   *go-nyo tsha-po.*

Intrigue   *tro-ngen.*

Intrinsic (real)   *ngo tho; nog-ne.*

Inundate, to   *chhu-yi nem-pa.*

Inundation   *chhu-ru.*

Invalid, s.   *ne-pa.*

Invective   *me-ra.*

Inveigle, to   *lu-wa.*

Inventory   *je-tho.*

Invert, to (back to front)   *kha-chho lok-pa.*

Invert, to (upside down)   *go-shu lok pa; a-lo gyap-pa.*

Investigate, to   *ship-cho che-pa.*

Investigation   *ship-cho.*

Invincible   *la...mi kha-wa.*

Invisible   *mi thong-wa.*

Invite, to (guest)   *ke-tang-wa.*

Invite, to (request)   *shu-wa.*

Involved (intricate)   *go-nyo tsha-po.*

Inward   *nang-ki.*

Irascible   *ru-ngar-po.*

Ire   *tshik-pa; khong-thro.*

Iris   *si-ling jang-pa.*

Irksome   *ka-le khak-po.*

Iron   *chaa.*

Iron, s.(for clothes)   *ur-te.*

Irrational   *ton-me.*

Irreligious, to be   *chho-sem me-pa.*

Irreparable, to be   *thap-me-pa.*

Irresistible, to be   *kak...mi thup-pa.*

Irresolute, to be   *ten-ten...me-po.*

Irritable   *ru-ngar-po.*

Irritate, to   *khong-thro lang-wa.*

Is   *re; du.*

Island   *ling-thren.*

Isolated place   *en-ne.*

Issue (result)   *nying-po.*

Issue, to (come out)   *thom-pa.*

It   *te; di.*

Itch, s.   *ngo.*

Itch, to (of body)   *sa-wa; ya-wa.*

Itching disease to have
   ngo-shor-wa; ngo-gyap-pa.

Itself   *di-rang; te-rang.*

Ivory   *pa-so.*

Ivy   *tha-khyu me-tok.*

J

Jackal   *khyip-chang.*

Jackass   *pung-gu.*

Jackdaw   *kyung-ka.*

Jacket (with sleeves)   *go-tse.*

Jacket, (without sleeves)   *ja-ja.*

Jade (stone)   *yang-tri.*

Jail   *tson-khang.*

Jailor   *tson-sung-nga.*

Jangle, to (wrangle)   *gyam-dre gyap-pa.*

January   *chin-dha dhang-po.*

Jar   *dza-pum.*

Jaundice   *tree-pa.*

Jaunt, to (ramble)
   chham-chham che-pa.

Javelin   *dung.*

Jaw   *dram-pa.*

Jealous   *thra-to tsha-po.*

Jealousy   *thra-to.*

Jeer, to   *kya-kya che-ne lap pa.*

Jelly (meat)   *phik-phi.*

Jest, to   *khap-le she-pa.*

Jester   *u-khor shu-khen.*

Jesus   *ye-shu.*

Jew   *ya-hu-da-pa.*

Jewel   *nor-pu.*

Jewellery   *gyen-chha.*

Job (work)   *le-ka.*

Jockey (for making horses)
   ta-jang-khen.

Join, to   *drel-wa; thu-pa.*

Join, to (by glueing together)
   jar-wa.

Joint, s.(of body)   *tshik.*

Jointly   *nyam-drel.*

Joke, to   *khap-le she-pa.*

Jollity   *ga-tshor.*

Jolly   *ga-po.*

Joss-stick   *po.*

Journey   *lang-ka.*

Joviality   *ga-tshor.*

Joviality, hon.   *nye-tshor.*

Joy   *ga-tshor.*

Joyful, to be   *ga-wa.*

Judge, to   *thrim-che-pa.*

Judge, s. (if a Chinaman)
   thrim-pon.

Judgement (legal)   *che-tsham;*
                      thra-ma.

Judgement (opinion)   *sam-pa.*

Judgement-hall   *le-khung.*

Jug   *chhu-no.*

Juggle, to (conjure)   *mik-thru tse pa.*

Juggler   *mik-thru tse-khen.*

Jugglery   *mik-thru.*

Juice   *khu-wa.*

July   *chin-dha dhun-pa.*

Jump, to   *chhong pa;*
             chhong-gya gyap-pa.

Junction of roads   *lam-dzom.*

June   *chin-dha dug-pa.*

Jungle   *shing-na.*

Juniper   *shuk-pa.*

Jurisdiction   *sa-ne.*

Just by   *tsa-la.*

Just now   *tan-da-rang.*

Just so ! (like that)   *ta-ka re.*

Just so! (like that) h.hon.   *la*
             ka nang-rang re.

Just, adj.   *thrim-trang-po.*

Just, adv.   *rang.*

Justice   *thrim trang-po.*

Justly   *thrim nang-shin.*

Jute   *so-ma ra-tsa.*

Juvenile   *shom pa; lo shon-shon.*

K

Kashmir   *Kha-chhe lungpa.*

Keen (eager)   *nying-do-po :*
             nying tro-po.

Keen (not blunt)   *no-po.*

Keep, to (have the care of)
             nyar-wa; cha-ka che-pa.

Keep, to (retain)   *shak-pa.*

Keeper (guard)   *sung-khen.*

Kennel   *khyi-tshang.*

Kerosene oil   *sa num.*

Kettle (for tea)   *kho-ti.*

Key   *di-mi*

Kham (province in Eastern Tibet)
             kham.

Kham, inhabitant of   *kham-pa.*

Kick   *dong-gya.*

Kick, to   *dong-gya shu-wa.*

Kid, s.   *re-ko.*

Kidney   *khay-ma.*

Kill, to   *se-pa.*

Kind, adj.   *trin chhem-po.*

Kind, different   *na-tsho.*

Kind, s.(sort)   *gyu.*

Kindle, to (fire)   *tang-wa.*

Kindly   *trin-chhem-po.*

Kindness   *trin.*

Kindred (relatives)   *nye-wa.*

Kindred (relatives) hon.
    ku-nyen.

King   *gye-po.*

King's business (administration)
    gye-si.

Kingdom   *gye-khap.*

Kiss, to   *kha-kyel-wa.*

Kitchen   *thap-tshang.*

Kitchen-garden   *tshe-yang-tse.*

Kite(bird)   *ping-kyu-ma.*

Kitten   *shim-thru.*

Knapsack   *to-phe.*

Knave   *ten-shi; dzap-chhen.*

Knee   *pee-mo.*

Knee-joint   *pi-mo tshik.*

Kneel, to   *pi mo tsuk-pa.*

Kneel, to hon.   *shap-pi tsuk-ka*
    nang-wa.

Knife   *tri.*

Knife   *di.*

Knife, clasp   *tap-tri.*

Knit, to   *le-wa.*

Knitting-needle   *chan-da.*

Knock, to   *tak-ta tang-wa.*

Knocking, s.   *tak-ta.*

Knot, s.   *du-pa.*

Knot, to   *du-pa gyap-pa.*

Knot, to untie a   *du-pa*
    shik-pa.

Know, to (persons)
    ngo-shem-pa.

Know, to (things)   *she-pa.*

Knowledge in general
    she-cha; yon-len.

Knuckle   *lak-pe tshik.*

L

Laborious (difficult)   *ka-le*
    khak-pa

Labour, to   *le-ka che-pa.*

Labour, forced   *u-la.*

Labourer   *mi la.*

Labourer's hire   *la.*

Lac (dye)   *gya-tsho.*

Lac (number)   *bum.*

Lacerate, to   *shak-pa.*

Lachery   *do-chha.*

Lack, to   *mi..tshang-wa.*

Lad   *pu-gu.*

Ladak (name of province)   *la-dak.*

Ladder   *ken-tsa.*

Lade, to   *khe kel-wa.*

Ladle, s.   *kyo.*

Ladle, to   *kyo-kyi luk-pa.*

Lady, young *se-mo.*

Lag, to *gor-wa.*

Lahoal (name of Province)
kar-sha.

Lair *tshang.*

Laity *a-u; jik-tem-pa.*

Lake *tsho.*

Lakh (number) *bum.*

Lama *la-ma.*

Lama, Grand (of Lhasa)
kyam-gon rim-po-chhe.

Lama, Grand (of Tashi Hlumpo)
pen-chhen rim-po-chhe.

Lamb *luk-thru; lu-ku.*

Lame *kang-kyo.*

Lamentation *nya-ngen.*

Lamp *shu-ma.*

Lamp (as offering to deity)
chho me.

Lance, s. *dung.*

Lancet *tsa-u.*

Land (earth) *sa.*

Landing-place *tru-kha.*

Landlady *ne-mo.*

Landlord *ne-po.*

Landlord (of land) *sa-i dak-po.*

Landslip *sa-ru.*

Landtax *sa-thre.*

Landuid *nyop-po.*

Lane *hrang-ga.*

Language *ke.*

Lantern *gang-shu.*

Lap up, to (water &c.) *dak-pa.*

Lap, s.(of women) *pang-pa.*

Lapsus linguae, to make a
kha-shor-wa.

Larch *sa-shing.*

Lard *phak tshi.*

Large *chhem-po.*

Large (of country, etc.)
gya-chhem-po.

Larynx *ke.*

Lascivious *do-chha chhem-po.*

Lasciviousness *do-chha.*

Lash (of a whip) *ta-cha.*

Lash, to *ta-cha shu-wa.*

Lass *pu-mo.*

Lassitude *ngel.*

Last night *dang-gong.*

Last year *da-nying.*

Last, to *thup-pa.*

Last, adj. *shuk-sho.*

Lasting (durable) *tro*
chhem-po.

Latch *a-shing.*

Latchet *hlam-dro.*

Late   *chhi-po.*

Late, to be   *chhi-po che-pa.*

Lately   *kha-sang.*

Latent   *be-pa.*

Later on   *shu-la.*

Latest   *shuk-sho.*

Latter   *shuk ma.*

Laud, to   *to-ra tang-wa.*

Laugh, s.   *ge-mo.*

Laughable   *ge-mo tro-po.*

Laughter   *ge-mo.*

Lavish (profuse)   *be pe; dzak-to.*

Law   *thrim.*

Law (religious)   *chho-thrim.*

Law-court   *thrim-sa.*

Law-suit   *kham-chhu.*

Lawful   *thrim-thun.*

Lawfully   *thrim-nang-shin.*

Lawless   *thrim-me.*

Lawn   *thang.*

Laws, to obey   *thrim khyer wa; thrim khur-wa.*

Lay the foundation of, to   *tsik-ten ting-wa.*

Lay, to (spread)   *ting-pa.*

Lay, to   *shak-pa.*

Lay, to (down)   *nye-wa.*

Lay, to (eggs)   *tang-wa.*

Lay, to (place)   *shak-pa.*

Layman   *a-u; jik-tem-pa.*

Lazy   *gyu ma ring-po : le-lo chhem-po.*

Lead (red-lead)   *sin-dhu-ra.*

Lead, s.(metal)   *sha-ni.*

Lead, to (away)   *thri-dro-wa.*

Lead, to (towards)   *thri-yong-wa.*

Leader   *go-pa.*

Leaf (of a tree)   *lo ma; da-ma.*

Leak, to (of water)   *dzak-pa.*

Lean, to (against)   *nye-de-pa.*

Lean, to (back)   *gyap-nye che-ne de-pa.*

Leap, to   *chhong-pa; chhong-gya gyap-pa.*

Learn, to   *lap-pa.*

Learn, to (by heart)   *lo-la sim-pa.*

Learner (novice)   *en-chhung.*

Learning   *she-cha; yon ten.*

Lease, s.   *ka-ten.*

Least   *chhung-sho.*

Leather   *ko-wa.*

Leave of absence   *gong-pa.*

Leave off, to (renounce)   *pang-wa.*

Leave, to (a country, etc.)   *sha-ne yong-wa.*

Leave, to (depart)   *thom-pa;*
                     chhim-pa.

Leave, to ask for   *gong pa*
                    shu-wa.

Leave, to grant   *gong-pa*
                  ter-wa.

Leaven (for fermenting liquor)
                     chhang-tsi.

Leaves (in a book)
                  shok-trang.

Leavings (things left)   *hla-ma.*

Lecherous   *do-chha chhem po.*

Leech   *pe-pa.*

Left (opp.to right)   *yon.*

Left, to be (behind)   *le-ne*
                       me-pa.

Left, to be (not expended)
                  hla-ma lu-pa.

Left-handed   *yon-la.*

Leg   *kang-pa.*

Leg (of mutton etc.)   *kang-sha.*

Legal   *thrim-thun.*

Legally   *thrim-nang-shin.*

Legend   *nam tha.*

Legged, bandy   *kang-kyo.*

Legible, to be   *lok-she-pa.*

Legitimate (lawful)   *thrim-thun.*

Legitimately   *thrim nang-shin.*

Leisure   *long.*

Leisure, to sit at   *hlo-hlo de-pa.*

Lend, to   *yar-wa.*

Length   *ring-thung.*

Length, at (afterwards)   *shu-la;*
                          je-la.

Lengthen, to   *ring tu tang-wa.*

Lengthy   *ring-po.*

Lenient, to be   *chha-yang*
                 nang-wa.

Leopard   *sik.*

Leper (male)   *dze-po.*

Leprosy   *dze.*

Less   *nyung-wa.*

Lessen, to (price)   *chak-pa.*

Lesson   *yi-gyuk.*

Let off, to   *tang-wa.*

Let, to (down)   *phap-pa.*

Letter (epistle)   *yi-ge.*

Level   *nyom-po.*

Lewd   *do-chha chhem-po.*

Lewdness   *do-chha.*

Lhasa   *hla-sa.*

Lhasa man, a   *hla-sa.*

Liar   *ham-pa sho-khen.*

Libation   *ser-kyem.*

Libel, s.   *me-ra.*

Liberal   *lak-pa shok-po.*

Liberate, to   *tang-wa.*

Liberated, to be   *thar-wa.*

Liberty   *tshe-thar.*

Libidinous   *do-chha chhem-po.*

Library   *pe-chha-khang.*

License   *ka-sho.*

Licentious   *do-chha chhem-po.*

Licentiousness   *do-chha.*

Lick, to (of animals)   *dak-pa.*

Lid   *khao-cho; kha.*

Lid (of the eye)   *mik-pa.*

Lie, to (down)   *nye-de-pa.*

Lie, to (tell untruth)   *nam-pa she-pa; kyak-dzun che-pa.*

Lie.s.   *ham-pa; kyak-dzun.*

Lieu of, in (instead of)   *tshap.*

Life   *so or hro; tshe.*

Life, to   *yar-kyak-pa; yar-lem-pa.*

Life-time   *tshe-kang.*

Light bulb   *log-gi shay-to.*

Light, adj. (not heavy)   *yang-po.*

Light, s.(brightness)   *o.*

Light, s.(lamp)   *shu-ma.*

Light, to (fire)   *tang-wa.*

Light, to (lamp)   *par-wa.*

Lightning (forked)   *khyu.*

Lightning, s.   *lo.*

Like (similar)   *nang-shin; dra-po.*

Like that   *ten-dra.*

Like this   *din-dra.*

Like, to   *ga-wa.*

Likeness (form)   *sop-ta.*

Likewise   *yang.*

Limb (of animals)   *suk-la.*

Limb (of human beings)   *suk-kyi yen-la.*

Lime   *sa-kar; kar-tsi.*

Limit   *tha.*

Limitation   *tsho.*

Limp, to   *kang-pa khyo-khyo che-pa.*

Limpid (clear)   *tang-po.*

Line   *thi.*

Line (in a book)   *yik-threng.*

Lineage (of laymen)   *ri-gyu; mi-gyu.*

Linen   *re.*

Linger, to   *gor-wa.*

Lining   *nang-sha.*

Link, to   *thu-gyap-pa.*

Lion   *seng-ge.*

Lioness   *seng-ge-mo.*

Lip   *chho-to.*

Lip, upper   *yen-chhu.*

Lip, lower   *men-chhu.*

Liquefy, to   *shu-wa.*

Liquid   *khu-wa.*

Liquid medicine   *thung-men.*

Liquor, distilled   *a-ra.*

List   *tho.*

Listen   *sen-dhang.*

Listen, to   *nyem-pa; am-chho nyem-pa.*

Literary language   *chho-ke.*

Literature   *chho.*

Little   *chhung-chhung.*

Little time, a   *hrip-tsa-chi.*

Little, a (few)   *tok-tsa; nyung-nyung.*

Live, adj.   *som-po.*

Live, to (dwell)   *de-pa.*

Lively   *hur-po; chang-po.*

Liver   *chhin-pa.*

Living, adj.   *som-pa.*

Lizard, sand (small)   *che-ma nyu-gu.*

Lizard, rock (large)   *tsam-pa kha-re.*

Lo !   *to-shi.*

Load (of an animal)   *khe; to-po.*

Load, to (a gun)   *dze-dzong gyap-pa.*

Load, to (animal)   *khe-ke-wa.*

Loadstone   *do-khap-len.*

Loaf   *pa-le.*

Loafer (tramp)   *gyeng-kham kor khen.*

Loan   *pu-lon.*

Loathe, to   *dang-po che-pa.*

Locality   *sa-chha.*

Lock, hon.   *sim-cha; chha-cha.*

Lock, s.   *gon-cha.*

Lock, to   *gon-cha gyap-pa.*

Locust   *a-tsha tshak-pa.*

Lodge   *ney-tshang.*

Lofty   *tho-po.*

Log (piece of wood)   *shing-tum.*

Loins   *ke-pa.*

Loiter, to   *gor-wa.*

Lonely   *chik-po.*

Lonely place   *en-ne.*

Long   *ring-po.*

Long for, to   *trem-pa.*

Long life, to have   *tshe-ring-wa.*

Long-lived   *tshe-ring-po.*

Look for, to (search)   *tsho-wa.*

Look, to   *ta-wa.*

Looking-glass   *she-go.*

Loom   *thak-thri.*

Loop   *lung.*

Loop-button   *thup-lung.*

Loose (not tight)   *lhu-lhu.*

Loose, to (liberate)   *tang-wa.*

Loose, to (slacken)   *hlo-hlo
tang-wa.*

Loosen, to   *lhu-lhu che-pa.*

Lord   *pom-po.*

Lose, to   *la-pa.*

Lose, to (in business)   *kyong
phok-pa.*

Lose, to (law-suit, etc.)   *shor-wa.*

Loss   *kyong.*

Loss of appetite   *tang-kha me-pa.*

Lost, it is   *la-ne min-du.*

Lot (fortune)   *so-de.*

Lot (many)   *mang-po.*

Lot (share)   *ke-la.*

Lots, to draw   *mo-gyap-pa.*

Lotus   *pe-ma.*

Loud (noisy)   *ke chhem-po.*

Louse   *shi.*

Love   *cham-po.*

Love, to   *cham-po che-pa.*

Lovely   *tshar-po; dze-po.*

Lover   *nying-du.*

Low   *ma-po.*

Low (cheap)   *khe-po.*

Low, to be (shallow)   *ting-ring-
po me-pa.*

Low-spirited, to be   *sem-kyo-
nang che-pa.*

Lower part of a thing   *me.*

Lower tooth   *me-so.*

Lowland   *me.*

Lowly   *sem-chhung-chhung.*

Loyal, to be   *ka-thun shu-wa.*

Lucid   *dra-tak-po.*

Luck (bad)   *so-de kam-po;
so-nam chhung-chhung*

Luck (good)   *so-de; so-nam.*

Lucky   *so-de chhem-po;
so-nam chhem-po.*

Ludicrous   *ge-mo tro-po.*

Luggage   *cha-la.*

Lugubrious, to be   *sem-kyo-wa;
sem-duk-pa.*

Lukewarm   *tron-jam.*

Lumbago, to have   *ke-pa na-wa.*

Luminous   *o chhem-po.*

Lump   *dok-do.*

Lunatic   *nyom-pa.*

Lunch   *nyin-gung kha-laa.*

Lungs   *lo.*

Lurk, to   *yip-ne de-pa.*

Lust   *do-chha.*

Lustful   *do-chha chhem-po.*

Lustre *si-ji; o.*

Lustrous *si-ji chhem-po; o chhem-po.*

Lusty *she chhem-po.*

Luxuriant *be-po.*

Lynx *i.*

M

Machine *so-khen.*

Machine, sewing *tshem-bu khor-lo.*

Mad *nyom-pa.*

Mad, to be *nyo-wa.*

Madam *cham-ku-sho.*

Magazine *dzo.*

Magic *mik-thru.*

Magician *mik-thru ton-khen.*

Magnanimity *trin.*

Magnanimous *trin chhem-po.*

Magnet *ngar-chaa.*

Magnificent *yang-dze.*

Magnitude *chhe-chhung.*

Magnolia *tsam-pa-ka.*

Magpie *tra-ka.*

Mahommedan *kha-chhe.*

Maid, maiden *pu-mo.*

Maid-servant *yo-mo.*

Main point *ton-nying.*

Mainly *phe-chher.*

Maintain, to (affirm) *lap-pa.*

Maintain, to (nourish) *so-wa.*

Maize *ken-dzom.*

Majestic *si-ji chhem-po.*

Majesty, his *rim-po-chhe.*

Major *ru-pon.*

Majority *mang-nga.*

Make, to *che-pa.*

Make, to (construct) *so-wa.*

Maker *so khen.*

Malady *na-tsha.*

Male *pho.*

Malefactor *dzap-chhen.*

Malice *no-sem.*

Malicious *sem ngem-po.*

Malign, to *me ra tang-wa.*

Malignant *sem ngem-po.*

Malignity *no-sem.*

Mallet *shing-ki tho-a.*

Maltreat, to *duk-po tang-wa.*

Mamma *a-ma.*

Mammon *nor-hla.*

Man *mi.*

Man-servant *yok-po.*

Manacles *lak-cha.*

Manage, to (superwise)	*to-tam che-pa.*	Mar, to	*kyon-che-pa.*
Manager to	*tam-pa*	March	*chin-dha sum-pa.*
Mandate	*ka.*	March, to	*dro wa.*
Mane (of horse, etc.)	*se.*	Mare	*go-ma.*
Mange	*ngo.*	Margin	*tha.*
Manger	*tre-ra.*	Marigold	*kur-kum me-to.*
Mangle, to (tear)	*kok-pa.*	Mark	*ta.*
Maniac	*nyom-pa.*	Mark, to (observe)	*mik-ta-wa.*
Manifest, adj.	*ngon-ne; ngo-tho.*	Marked (famous)	*ke-tra chhem-po.*
Manifold	*na-tsho.*	Market	*trom.*
Mankind	*mi-ri.*	Marriage	*chhang-sa.*
Manly (brave)	*nying-chhem-po lo-kho chhem po.*	Marry, to (take a husband)	*mak-pa lang-wa.*
Manner (custom)	*luk-so.*	Marry, to (take a wife)	*na-ma lem-pa.*
Manoeuvre, to (troops)	*ma-jong che-pa.*	Mart	*throm.*
Mansion	*sim-sha; pho-trang.*	Marvel, s.	*yam tshen.*
Mantle	*chhu-pa.*	Marvel, to	*khye-tsha-po che-pa.*
Manufacture, to	*so-wa.*	Marvellous	*yam-tshem-po; khye-tsha-po.*
Manure	*lu.*	Mask	*ba.*
Manuscript	*tri-ma.*	Mason	*dop-so-wa.*
Many	*mang-po.*	Masquerade	*chham.*
Many (very)	*ha chang mang-po; yo-ma-su.*	Massage, to	*phu-phu che-pa.*
Many, how	*ka-tsho.*	Massive (bulky)	*bom-po.*
Many, too	*hlak-po.*	Mast (flag-staff)	*tar-po-chhe.*
Map	*sab-ta.*	Master	*jin-da; dak-po.*

Mastery (power)   *wang.*

Mastiff   *drok-khyi.*

Mat   *den.*

Match (lucifer)   *mu-si.*

Match-box   *mu-si gam-chhung.*

Matches   *tsag-da.*

Mate   *ro.*

Material, s.   *gyu.*

Maternal aunt   *su-mo.*

Matter (substance)   *gyu.*

Mattress   *bo-den.*

Mature, to be   *tsho-pa.*

Maxim   *tam-pe.*

May   *chin-dha nga-pa.*

Me   *nga-la.*

Meadow   *pang.*

Meagre (lean)   *sha-kam-po.*

Meagre (scanty)   *nyung-nyung.*

Meal (food taken at one time)
    kha-la; to; top-chhe.

Mean (stingy)   *lak-pa tam-po.*

Mean (vulgar)   *kyu-ma.*

Mean, to (purpose)   *sem-la
        sam-pa.*

Meaning   *ton-ta.*

Means, by what   *kan-dre.*

Means, by all   *nge-par.*

Means, s.   *thap.*

Meantime, in the   *khap-su.*

Meanwhile, in the   *khap-su.*

Measles   *si-bi.*

Measure, s.   *tshe.*

Measure, to   *je-wa.*

Meat   *sha.*

Mediate, to   *par-mi che-pa.*

Mediator   *par-mi che-khen.*

Medicine   *men.*

Medicine for internal use   *khong-
        men.*

Medicine, mineral   *sa-men.*

Meditate, to   *sam-pa.*

Meditate, to (on religious affairs)
        gom-gyap-pa.

Meditation, religious   *ting-nge
        dzin.*

Medium (of quality)
        dring-chi; thrik-thri-chi.

Meek   *sem chhung-chhung.*

Meek in speech   *kha jam-po.*

Meet, to   *thuk-pa.*

Meeting   *thuk-thre.*

Megistrate, city (chinaman)
        thrim-pon.

Melancholy, to be   *sem-kyo-nang
        che-pa.*

Melt, to   *shu-wa.*

Memoir (story)   *nam-tha.*

Memory   *trem-pa.*

Menace, to   *dzik-dzik tang-wa.*

Mend, to   *drok-pa.*

Mend, to (by patching)

     hlem-pa gyap-pa.

Mendacious, to be   *ham-pa sho-pa; kyak-dzun sho-pa.*

Mendicant   *pang-ko.*

Menses   *da-tshen.*

Menstruate, to   *da-thra, gyap-pa.*

Mention, to   *lap-pa.*

Merchandise   *tshong-so.*

Merchant   *tshong-pa.*

Merciful   *nying-je chhem-po.*

Merciless, to be   *nying-je me-pa.*

Mercury   *ngu-chhu.*

Mercy   *nying-je.*

Mercy, hon.   *thuk-je.*

Merely   *sha-ta.*

Merit   *ge-wa : tsho.*

Merit, to   *o-pa.*

Merriment   *ga-tshor.*

Merry, to be   *ga-wa; kyi-po che-ne do-pa.*

Message   *len.*

Messenger   *pang-chhen.*

Method (means)   *thap.*

Mewing, s.(of cat)   *me-o.*

Mid-day   *nyin-kung.*

Middle of, in the   *kyi-la.*

Middle, adj.   *dring-chi; thrik-thri-chi.*

Middle, s.   *kyi.*

Midnight   *nam-chhe.*

Midst, in the   *kyi-la.*

Mien   *sop-ta.*

Might (official authority)   *wang.*

Might (physical)   *she.*

Mighty (officially)   *wang chhem-po.*

Mighty (physically)   *she chhem-po.*

Milch cow   *sho-ma.*

Mild (of climate)   *si-tro nyom-po.*

Mild in speech   *kha jam-po.*

Mild in speech, hon.   *she jam-po.*

Militia (first) see "army"   *dom-ma.*

Milk   *wo-ma.*

Milk, to   *sho-wa.*

Milk-jug   *o-no.*

Million   *sa-ya.*

Mimic, to   *len-to che-pa.*

Mimicry   *len-to.*

Mina (bird)   *me-na.*

Mince, to   *tsap-pa.*

Mind   *lo; sem.*

Mind ! never   *a-u-tse.*

Mind, to (take care of)   *nyar-wa.*

Mine, pron.   *nge.*

Minister, chief   *lon-chhen.*

Mint   *ngu-par-khang.*

Minute (time)   *kar-ma.*

Minute, adj.   *ship-ship.*

Miracle   *yam-tshen.*

Miraculous   *yam-tshem po; khye-tsha-po.*

Mire   *dam; dzap.*

Mirror   *she-go.*

Mirth   *ga-tshor.*

Mirthful, to be   *ga-wa.*

Mischief   *kyon.*

Miscreant   *dzap-chhen.*

Miserable (unappy)   *dung-nge chhem-po.*

Miserliness   *ser-na.*

Miserly   *ser-na chhem-po.*

Misery   *dung-nge.*

Misfortune   *so-de kam-po.*

Mist   *muk-pa.*

Mistake in speech, to make a   *kha-nor-wa.*

Mistake, to   *nor-wa.*

Mistified, to be   *go-thom-pa.*

Misunderstood, to be   *ko-lok chung-wa.*

Mock to   *kya-kya che-ne lap-pa.*

Mode (custom)   *luk-so.*

Model   *pe.*

Modelled well   *bo-pa to-po.*

Moderate, to be   *tsho-sim-pa.*

Modern   *te-ring sang-ki.*

Modest, to be   *ma-sa sim-pa.*

Mohammadan   *kha-chhe.*

Moist   *lom-pa.*

Moisten, to   *bang-wa.*

Moisture(of ground)   *sha-tshen.*

Molar rooth   *dram-so.*

Mole   *men.*

Molest, to   *duk-po tang-wa.*

Moment (importance)   *nen-kha.*

Moment, in a   *hrip-tsa-chi.*

Momentous   *nen-kha chhem-po; ke chhem po.*

Monarch   *gye-po.*

Monarch's administration   *gye-si.*

Monastery   *gon-pa.*

Monday   *sa-da-wa.*

Monday   *za dha-wa.*

Money   *ngu.*

Mongol, Mongolian   *sok-po.*

Monk   *da-pa.*

Monkey   *pe-u.*

Monstrous (horrible)   *she-tra tsha-po.*

Monstrous (huge)   *chhe-thak-chho.*

Month   *da-wa.*

Month, Ist half of   *da-to; tshe-shar.*

Moon   *da-wa.*

Moonlight   *da-ka.*

Moral, adj.(of persons)   *tshun-den.*

Morality   *tshu-thrim.*

More   *mang-nga; hlak-ka.*

Moreover   *tan-do.*

Morning   *shok-ke; nga-tro.*

Morrow   *sang-nyi.*

Morsel, a   *tak-ka-chi.*

Mortal, s.   *mi.*

Mortar (for pounding)   *gok-ting.*

Mortification (shame)   *ngo-tsha.*

Mortified, to feel   *ngo-tsha-wa.*

Mosquito   *tuk-drang.*

Most   *mang-sho.*

Most part, for the   *phe-chher.*

Moth   *chhem-drem-ma.*

Mother   *a-ma.*

Mother   *a-ma-laa.*

Mother of pearl   *nyap-chhi.*

Motive   *ton-to.*

Mould (for shaping)   *pan.*

Mouldy, to be   *ham-pa gyap-pa.*

Mound   *sa-phung.*

Mount for photograph   *par-kyi gyap-sha shok-ku.*

Mount, to (climb)   *dzak-pa.*

Mount, to (rise)   *lang-wa.*

Mountain   *ri.*

Mountain-pass   *la.*

Mouse   *tsi-tsi.*

Moustache   *a-ra.*

Mouth   *kha.*

Mouthful   *kham-do-chi.*

Move, to (go)   *dro-wa.*

Move, to (persuade)   *lap-cha che-po.*

Mow, to   *nga-wa.*

Much (many)   *mang po.*

Much, too   *hlak-pa; hla-ma.*

Much, very   *ha-chang mang-po.*

Mud   *dam; dzap.*

Muddy (of water)   *nyok-po.*

Muhammadan   *kha-chhe.*

Mule   *tre.*

Mule, baggage   *khe-tre.*

Mule, riding   *shon-tre.*

Muleteer   *tre-pa.*

Multitude of men   *mi-tsha.*

Mumps   *dram-pa trang-wa.*

Murder, to   *se-pa.*

Murderer   *mi-se-khen.*

Murky, to become (from clouds)
                              thip-pa.

Muscle   *tsa.*

Muse, to (meditate)   *sam-pa.*

Museum   *dem-ton-khang.*

Mushroom (two kinds)   *ka-sha;*
                              sh-sha.

Musk   *la-tsi.*

Musk-deer   *la-wa.*

Musket   *men-da.*

Musket-ball   *di-u.*

Muslim   *kha-chhe.*

Must, v.i.   *go-wa.*

Mustard   *pe-kang.*

Muster, to, v.i.   *tshok-pa; dzom-pa.*

Musty, to be   *ham-pa gyap-pa.*

Mute, to be (silent)   *kha-kha*
                              de-pa.

Mute, s. (dumb person)   *kuk-pa.*

Mutton   *luk-sha.*

My   *nge.*

Myrabolam   *a-ru.*

Myrrh   *a-ka-ru.*

Myself   *nga-rang.*

Myth   *drum.*

N

Nail   *ser.*

Nail, iron   *chak-ser.*

Nail, to   *chak-ser gyap-pa.*

Nail, toe   *kang-pe se-mo.*

Naked   *mar-hrang-nga.*

Name   *ming.*

Name, to   *ming dok-pa.*

Nap (sleep)   *nyi.*

Napkin   *pang-khep.*

Narrate, to   *she-pa.*

Narrative   *gyu-kyen; lo-gyu.*

Narrow   *tok-po; bu-su tok-po.*

Nasty   *kyuk-tro-po.*

Nation   *mi-gyu; ri-gyu.*

Native land   *kye-sa.*

Nature (species)   *gyu.*

Naught (cipher)   *le-kor.*

Naughty   *ngem-pa.*

Nauseating   *kyuk-tro-po.*

Navel   *te.*

Near   *nye-po*

Nearly (almost)   *ha-lam; ka-chhen.*

Neat   *dra-chhak-po.*

Necessary   *go-pa.*

Necessity   *go-pa; kho-chhe.*

Neck   *ke.*

Neck, back of   *jing-pa.*

Necklace   *kye-gyen.*

Nectar   *du-tsi.*

Need, s.(necessity)   *go-pa;*
   kho-chhe.

Need, to (require)   *go-pa.*

Needful   *go-pa.*

Needfulness   *go-pa; kho-chhe.*

Needle   *khap.*

Needle, eye of   *khap-mi.*

Needle, point of   *khap-tse.*

Needy (poor)   *kyo-po; nyem chhung.*

Nefarious   *ngem-po.*

Negotiate, to   *drik-chha che-pa.*

Negotiation   *ka-mon; drik-chha.*

Neigh, to   *ta-ke gyap-pa.*

Neighbour   *khyim-tshe.*

Neighbourhood   *nye-khor.*

Nepal   *pe-yu.*

Nepalese   *pe-po.*

Nephew   *tsha-wa.*

Nerve   *chhu-gyu.*

Nest   *tshang.*

Net   *gya; tra-a.*

Nettle, s.   *sa-po.*

Nettle, to (irritate)   *khong-thro*
   lang-wa.

Neuralgia   *ya-ma.*

Never   *tsa-ne..ma; ma-ne...ma.*

Never mind !   *a-u-tse.*

Nevertheless   *yin-ne; yin-kyang;*
   yin-na-yang.

New   *sa-pa.*

New year   *lo-sa.*

News   *ne-tshu; sang-gyu.*

Newspaper   *tshag-paa.*

Next   *je-may.*

Next (at the side of)   *tsa;*
   dram-la.

Nice (accurate)   *thrik-thrik;*
   ten-ten.

Nice (in favour)   *shim-po.*

Nice (pleasant)   *tar-po; yak-po.*

Nickname   *ming-do; ming ngen.*

Niece   *tsha-mo.*

Niggardly   *lak-pa tam-po.*

Night   *tshen; gong-mo.*

Night, last   *dang-gong.*

Nimble   *hur-po; gyok-po.*

Nine   *gu.*

Nineteen   *chu-gu.*

Nineteenth   *chu-gu-pa.*

Ninetieth   *gup-chu-pa.*

Ninety   *gup-chu tham-pa.*

Ninny   *kuk-pa; lem-pa.*

Ninth   *gu-pa.*

Nipple (of breast)   *o-me-tse; nu-sor.*

No   *ma-rey, meyn, min-dhoo.*

Noble, s.   *ku-tra.*

Nobleman   *ku-tra.*

Nobody   *su-yang (w.neg.)*

Nod, to   *go jok-jok che-pa.*

Noise   *u-dra.*

Noise, to make a   *u-dra gyap-pa.*

Noisome   *kyuk-tro-po.*

Nomad   *drok-pa.*

Nominate, to   *ko-wa.*

None (nobody)   *su-yang (w.neg.)*

Nonsensical   *ton-me.*

Nook   *sur.*

Noon   *nyin-kung.*

Noose   *shak-pa.*

North   *chang.*

Northward   *chang-ngo; chang-chho.*

Nose   *na-khu.*

Nose   *na-gu.*

Nose bleeding   *na-traa.*

Nostril   *na-khung.*

Not   *ma; mi.*

Not at all   *tsa-ne (w.neg.)*

Notable (celebrated)   *nyen-tra chhem-po.*

Note, s. (letter)   *yi-ge.*

Note, s. (reputation)   *ke-tra.*

Note, to (observe)   *mik-ta-wa.*

Notebook   *di-dheb.*

Noted   *ke-tra chhem-po.*

Nothing   *ka-ke (w.neg.)*

Notice   *len.*

Notice, to (mention)   *lap-pa.*

Notice, to (see)   *mik-ta-wa.*

Notification (of government)   *ka-gya.*

Notion (opinion)   *sam-pa.*

Notorious   *ke-tra chhem-po.*

Notwithstanding   *yin-ne; yin-kyang; yin-na-yang.*

Noun   *ming-dra.*

Nourish, to   *so-wa.*

Novel, (new)   *sa-pa.*

November   *chin-dha chu-chig*

Novice, religious   *ge-tshu.*

Now (at this time)   *tan-da.*

Now (well, yes)   *o-na.*

Now and then   *tsham-tsham.*

Now-a-days   *te-ring-sang; teng-sang.*

Nowhere *ka-pa...ma; ka-re...ma.*

Noxious *kyuk-tro-po.*

Nude *mar-hrang-nga.*

Nullify, to *me-pa so-wa.*

Number (numeral) *trang-ka; ang-ki.*

Number, to *trang-ka gyap-pa.*

Numberless *trang-me.*

Numerous *mang-po.*

Numerous, very *yo-ma-su.*

Nun *a-ni.*

Nuptials *chhang-sa.*

Nurse (of children) *u-dzi; pu-dzi.*

Nurture, to *so-wa.*

Nutmeg *dza-ti.*

Nutrition *kha-la; to.*

O

O clock *chhu-tsho.*

Oar *tru-kya.*

Oath *na.*

Oath, to takean *na kyel-wa.*

Obdurate, to be (obstinate) *kyong-po.*

Obdurate, to be (hard-hearted) *nying-je me-pa.*

Obedient *kha-la nyem-po.*

Obeisance, to make (by kneeling) *chha-tshe-wa.*

Obeisance, to make (by prostration) *chha-tshe-wa.*

Obeisance, to make (by raising hand) *chham-bu shu-wa.*

Obese *sha-gyak-pa.*

Obey laws, to *thrim khyer-wa; thrim khur-wa.*

Obey, to *kha-la nue..i-pa.*

Object (intention) *ton-ta.*

Object, to *kak-pa.*

Obliged, to be (thankful) *trin trem-pa.*

Obliging *trin chhem-po.*

Obligue *kyok-kyo.*

Obliterate, to *sup-pa.*

Obscure (dark) *nak-po.*

Obscurity (darkness) *min-na.*

Observe, to *mik-ta-wa.*

Obstacle *kak-chha.*

Obstinate *kyong-po.*

Obstruct, to *kak pa.*

Obtain, to *jor-wa; thop-pa.*

Obtuse (dull) *kuk-pa; lem-pa.*

Occasion (cause) *kyen; gyu-kyen.*

Occasionally *tsham-tsham.*

Occupation *le-ka.*

Occupied with work, to be
         tre-wa yo-pa.

Occur, to   *yong-wa.*

Ocean   *gyam-tsho.*

October   *chin-dha chu-pa.*

Odd (not a pair)   *ya-chi.*

Odious   *kyuk-tro-po.*

Odour   *tri-ma.*

Odour, to have   *tri-ma kha-wa.*

Of, past.   *ki; kyi; kyi.*

Off, adv.   *ne.*

Offal   *tsok-pa.*

Offence (anger)   *tshik-pa;*
         khong-thro.

Offence, to commit   *nye-pa*
         sak-pa.

Offence, to give   *khong-thro*
         lang-wa.

Offence, to take   *tsher-wa.*

Offend, to   *mam-be che-pa.*

Offensive (disgusting)   *kyuk-tro-po.*

Offer, to   *ter-wa.*

Offering   *chho-bul.*

Offering (presents)   *bul-wa.*

Office   *le-khung.*

Office (employment)   *le-ka.*

Office-room   *yik-tshang.*

Officer   *pom-po.*

Official   *pom-po.*

Officiate, to   *le-tshap che-pa.*

Offspring   *pu-gu.*

Often   *tshar mang-pe.*

Oh !   *a-kha-kha.*

Oil   *num.*

Ointment   *chuk-pa.*

Old (persons & animals)   *ga-pu.*

Old (of things)   *nying-pa.*

Old man   *ga-pu.*

Old woman   *ga-mu.*

Old, to grow   *ge-pa.*

Omen   *tem-dre.*

Omit, to   *sup-pa.*

On   *gdng-la; teng-la.*

Once   *tshar-chi; theng-chi.*

Once, at (immediately)   *lam-sang.*

One   *chig.*

One hundred   *gya tham-pa.*

One thousand   *tong-tra chig.*

One-eyed   *shar-ra; mik-shar.*

Onion   *tsong.*

Only (alone)   *chik-po.*

Onward (forward)   *ngen-la.*

Open (frank)   *trang-po.*

Open, to   *kha-chhe-pa.*

Opening   *i-khung.*

Openly (frankly)   *ma...sang-wa.*

Operation   *tri-shak-pa.*

Opinion   *sam-pa.*

Opium   *ya-phin; nye-tha-kha.*

Opponent   *dra.*

Opportunity   *thap.*

Oppose, to (dispute)   *tso-pa gyap-pa.*

Oppose, to (thwart)   *kak-pa.*

Opposite side   *pha-chho.*

Opposite, (different)   *mi chik-pa.*

Oppress, to (press against)   *nem-pa.*

Oppress, to (use severely)   *duk-po tang-wa; sop-ta so-wa.*

Opthalmia   *mik-ne.*

Optical deception   *mik-thru.*

Option   *thang.*

Opulent   *chhuk-po; cha-la chhem-po.*

Opulent, hon.   *ku-che chhem-po.*

Oracle (prophecy)   *tung-ten.*

Oral   *khe.*

Orally   *kha-ne.*

Orange   *li-wang.*

Orchard   *dum-ra.*

Order (rank)   *ko-sa; ko-ne; rim-pa.*

Order to, in   *ton-la.*

Order, s.(command)   *ka.*

Order, to   *ka-nang-wa.*

Ordert, to (things from shop)   *ngak-pa.*

Ordinarily   *phe-chher.*

Ordinary (in quality)   *kyu-ma.*

Orifice   *i-khung.*

Origin   *chung-tang.*

Ornament   *gyen-chha.*

Orphan   *ta-thru.*

Orthography   *tak-yi.*

Ostentatious   *nyam-to-po.*

Other   *shem-pa; yem-pa.*

Otter   *hram.*

Ought   *go-pa.*

Our   *nga-tsho.*

Out (outside)   *chhi-lo-la.*

Out of   *ne.*

Outcry   *u-dra.*

Outlet   *go.*

Outside, adv.   *chhi-lo-la.*

Outward   *chhi-i.*

Oven   *thap.*

Over (above)   *ya-ke.*

Overbear, to   *gye-wa; la khe-pa.*

Overbearing   *nyam-chhem-po; dza-kho chhem-po.*

Overcome, to	*gye-wa; la khe-pa.*
Overflow, to	*lu-pa.*
Overpower, to	*gye-wa; la khe-pa.*
Overtake, to	*je-sim pa.*
Overthrow, to	*gye-wa.*
Overturn, to	*go-shu lok-pu; a-lo gyap-pa.*
Owe to	*pu-lon suk-pa.*
Owl	*uk-pa.*
Own, adj.	*rang-ki.*
Owner	*dak-po.*
Ox	*lang; lang-ko.*

P

Pace (stride)	*kom-pa.*
Paces (of a horse)	*dro.*
Pack (load)	*khe.*
Pack on, to (load)	*kel-wa.*
Pack-horse	*khe-ta.*
Pack-mule	*khe-tre.*
Pack-pony	*khe-ta.*
Pack-saddle	*ga.*
Packet of paper, large.	*shok-dri.*
Padlock	*go-cha.*
Page of book	*shok-le.*
Pail (of wood)	*so-la.*

Pain (punishment by beating)	*thrim.*
Pain, bodily	*su.*
Pain, mental	*dung-nge.*
Painful	*suk-chhem-po.*
Painstaking	*nying-ru chhem-po.*
Paint, s.	*tshon.*
Paint, to (cover with colour)	*tshon tang-wa.*
Paint, to (picture)	*tri-pa.*
Painter	*hlap-ri-pa.*
Painting	*ri-mo.*
Pair	*chha.*
Palace	*pho-trang.*
Palace	*pho-dang.*
Palanquin	*gyo-chang.*
Palate	*ken.*
Pale	*kar-po kar-kyang.*
Pallid	*kar-po kar-kyang.*
Palm	*lag-thi.*
Palsy	*trum-pu chhu-se.*
Paltry	*ton-ta chhung-chhung.*
Pan	*la-nga.*
Pang (of grief)	*dung-nge.*
Pang, mental	*du-nge.*
Pang, physical	*su.*
Pankah	*lung-yap.*
Pant, to	*ngam-pa.*

Pant, to (for breath)   *u sak-pa.*

Pantaloons   *ko-thung; tor-ma.*

Panther   *sik.*

Pantry   *nyer-tshang.*

Paper   *shu-gu.*

Parable   *pe; dra-pe.*

Paradise   *de-wa-chen-kyi shing-kham*

Parasol   *nyi-du.*

Parcel   *par-sal.*

Parcel out, to   *go-pa : gop-sha gyap-pa.*

Parcel(round)   *thum-ti.*

Parched (dry)   *kam-po.*

Pardon   *gong-pa.*

Pare, to   *pak-pa shu-wa.*

Parents   *pha-ma.*

Park   *ling-ka.*

Park   *ling-ka.*

Parrot   *a-u-nen tso nen-tso.*

Parsimonious   *lak-pa tam-po.*

Part   *tum-pu.*

Part, to   *kha-kye-pa.*

Partial, to be (biassed)   *nye-ring-che-pa.*

Particular (exact)   *thrik-thrik : ten-ten.*

Particularly   *khye-par-tu.*

Partly   *tok-lsa.*

Partner (in business)   *tshong-ro*

Party (faction)   *chho.*

Pass the time, to   *go-khor-wa.*

Pass, s.(over mountains)   *la.*

Pass, to (go), v.i.   *dro-wa.*

Passenger (traveller)   *dru-pa.*

Passion (lust)   *do-chha.*

Passion (rage)   *tshik-pa; khong-thro.*

Passionate   *ru-ngar-po.*

Passport   *paa-si.*

Pastime (game)   *tse-mo.*

Pastry-puff   *mo mo.*

Patch, s.   *hlem-pa.*

Patch, to   *hlem-pa gyap pa.*

Path   *lang-ka.*

Path (by cliff)   *thrang.*

Patience (forwbearance)   *so-pa.*

Patient, to be (to endure)   *so-pa gom pa.*

Patiently, to wait   *gu de-pa.*

Patron   *gon-dren nang-khen.*

Patronage   *gon-dren.*

Patronize, to   *gon-dren nang-wa.*

Pattern   *pe.*

Pauper   *nyem chhung; kyo-po.*

Pav   *la; pho.*

Paw   *der-mo.*

Pawn, to   *ta-ma shak-pa.*

Pay back, to   *kyin tshap tre-pa.*

Pay taxes, to   *thre je-wa.*

Pay, to   *la-tre-pa; pho-tre-pa.*

Paymaster   *pho-pon.*

Pea   *trem-ma.*

Peace   *kyi-po; tu de-po.*

Peach   *kham-pu.*

Peacock   *màp-cha.*

Peak (of mountain)   *tse.*

Pear   *li.*

Pearl   *mu-tig.*

Peasant   *so-nam che-kher.*

Pebble   *do-hru.*

Peculiar   *khye-tsha po; yam-tshem-po.*

Pedestrian   *kang-thang-nga.*

Peel, s   *pak-pa.*

Peel, to   *pak pa shu-wa.*

Peg, iron   *cha-phu.*

Pegan   *chhi-pa.*

Pelt, to (stone)   *shu-wa.*

Pen   *nyu-gu.*

Penalty   *chhe-pa; nye-pa.*

Pencil   *zha-nyu.*

Pending   *ma-tshar-wa.*

Penetrate, to (enter)   *dzu-wa.*

Penis   *je lig-pa.*

Penurious   *kyo-po; nyem-chhung.*

People   *mi.*

Pepper   *pho-wa ri-pu.*

Peradventure   *chik-che-na.*

Perceive, to (understand)
    she-pa; ha-ko-ya.

Perceive, to (with the eye)
    thong-wa.

Percept (maxim)   *tam-pe.*

Perfect   *phun-sum tshok-pa.*

Perform, to   *che-pa.*

Perfume   *tri-ma.*

Perhaps   *chig-jey-na.*

Peril   *nyen-kha.*

Perilous   *nyen-kha chhem-po.*

Period   *tu, kel-pa.*

Perish, to   *shi-wa.*

Permission   *gong-pa.*

Permit, to   *chuk-pa.*

Perpetual   *gyun-chhe-gyu me-pa.*

Perpetually   *nam-gyun : tu-gyun.*

Perplexed, to be   *go-thom-pa.*

Perplexing   *go-nyo tsha-po.*

Perplexity   *go-nyo.*

Persecute, to   *no-pa che-pa.*

Persecution   *no-pa.*

Perseverance	nying-ru.	Phthisis	chong-ne.
Persevere, to	nying-ru che-pa.	Physic	men.
Persia	ta-si.	Physician	am-chhi.
Persian	ta sik-pa.	Pick up, to	ya-druk-pa; ya-khyak-pa.
Persist, to	u tshu che=pa.		
Persistence	u tshu.	Pick, to (a quarrel)	nye-ko-wa.
Person	mi.	Pick, to (flowers, etc.)	tok-pa.
Personally	rang.	Pictorial representation	ri-mo.
Perspiration	ngu-na.	Picture	thang-ka.
Perspire, to	ngu-na thom-pa.	Piebald (horse)	tap-thra.
Persuade, to	lap-cha che-pa.	Piece	tum-pu.
Persue, to	lok-pa.	Pierce, to	phi-pa.
Perverse	kyong-po.	Piety	chho-sem; ge-sem.

Pessimistic, to be (hopeless)
                    re-wa me-pa.

		Pig	phak-pa.
Pestle	ya-gya; ting-ri.	Pig-sty	phak-tshang.
Pet, to	che-po che-pa.	Pig-tail	chang-lo.
		Pigeon	ang-ku.
Petition	nye-shu.	Pike (spear)	dung.
Petroleum	sa-num.	Pile, to	pung-ne shak-pa.
Petticoat	me-yo.	Piles	trang-thor.

Petty (matter)	ton-ne chhung-chhung.	Pilgrim	ne-kor-ra.
		Pilgrimage	ne-kor.
Pewter	tik-tsha.	Pill	ri-pu.
Phantom	dong-dre; dre.	Pillage, to (rob)	chak-pa gyap-pa.
Pheasant, Blood	se-mo.	Pillar	ka-a.
Phlegm	lu-pa.	Pillow	ngey-go.
Photographic mount	par-kyi gyap-sha shok-ku.	Pillow case	ngey-shub.

Pimple   *thor-pa*

Pin   *ser.*

Pincers   *kam-pa.*

Pinch, to   *sem-tho gyap-pa.*

Pinch, to (twisting the skin)
   shap-chu gyap-pa.

Pine-tree (pinus Excelsa)
   thang-shing.

Pink   *zing-kya.*

Pinnacle   *hla-tsuk; cho.*

Pious   *chho-sem chhem-po.*

Pipe (musical instrument)
   ling-pu.

Pipe (tobacco)   *kang-sa.*

Pistol   *trom-da.*

Pit   *sa-tong; tong.*

Pitch (of the voice)   *dang.*

Pitcher   *chhu-no; chhu-pen.*

Pitiless, to be   *nying je....me-pa.*

Pity   *nying-je; cham-nying-je.*

Place in, to   *chuk-pa.*

Place, s   *sa-chha.*

Place, to   *shak-pa.*

Placenta   *sha-ma.*

Plague   *nyen-ne.*

Plain   *thang.*

Plain paper   *thig-mey shu-gu.*

Plain, adj.(clear)   *se-po.*

Plaintiff   *shu-tuk che po.*

Plait (of hat)   *chang-lo.*

Plan (pattern)   *ri-mo.*

Plane   *bu-hlen.*

Plane, to   *bu-hlen gyap-pa.*

Planet   *sa.*

Plank   *pang-le.*

Plant, to   *tsuk-pa.*

Plantain   *kye-dong.*

Plate   *tha-pa.*

Play   *tse-mo.*

Play, to   *tse mo tse-wa.*

Play-fellow   *tse-ro.*

Plea (controversy)   *lap-shi;
   tso-pa.*

Plead, to   *shu-wa.*

Pleader   *par-mi che-khen.*

Pleasant   *kyi-po.*

Please   *thu-je zig, ku-kyi.*

Please, if you   *ro nang;
   ro-che.*

Pleased, to be   *ga-wa.*

Pleasure   *ga-tshor.*

Pledge   *ta-ma.*

Plenteons   *be-po; dzak-to.*

Plentiful   *be-po; dzak-to.*

Pliable   *nyem-po.*

Pliant (flexible)   *nyem-po.*

Plough, to   *mom-pa gyap-pa.*

Plough, s   *sho.*

Ploughman   *mom-pa gyang-khen; thon-khen.*

Pluck, to (from tree)   *tok-pa.*

Plump   *sha-gyak-pa.*

Plunder, to (by stealth)   *ku-wa.*

Pneumonia   *pe-thra.*

Pocket   *am-pa.*

Pocket-mark   *bar-tsa.*

Pod   *kam-pu.*

Poem   *nye-nga.*

Poet   *nye-nga tri-khen.*

Point out, to (idicate)   *mi-tom-pa.*

Point(of nail)   *tse.*

Poised evenly, to be   *yang-ji me-pa.*

Poison   *tu.*

Policeman   *ko-chak-pa.*

Policy   *luk-so.*

Polite language   *she-sa.*

Pollute, to   *tsok-pa so-wa.*

Pollution   *trip.*

Pond   *chhu-khyil.*

Ponder, to   *sam-lo tang-wa.*

Ponderous (heavy)   *ji-po.*

Pony   *ta.*

Pony, pack   *khe-ta.*

Pony, riding   *shon-ta.*

Pool (small)   *chhu-khyil.*

Poor   *kyo-po; nyem-chhung.*

Poplar   *ja-pa.*

Poppy   *tom-den me to.*

Population   *mi-trang.*

Porch   *chhi-go.*

Porcupine   *sik-mo.*

Pork   *phak-sha.*

Porridge   *pa-thu.*

Portent   *tem-dre.*

Portion   *ke-la.*

Position (in society)   *gyu.*

Positive   *ten-ten.*

Possessor   *dak-po.*

Possible, to be   *thup-pa.*

Post (pillar)   *ka-a.*

Postage stamp   *ti-ka-si dag-tham.*

Posterior (anus)   *kup.*

Postman   *dag-pa.*

Postoffice   *da-khang.*

Postpone, to (adjourn)   *shak-pa.*

Posture   *dap.*

Pot   *kho-ma.*

Potato   *zho-kho.*

Potency   *wang.*

Potter   *dza-khen.*

Pouch (for tobacco)	*tha-khu.*
Pound, to (crush)	*dzok-pa.*
Pour, to	*luk-pa.*
Powder	*chhe-ma.*
Power (official)	*wang.*
Power (physical)	*she.*
Powerful (officially)	*wang chhem-po.*
Powerful (physically)	*she chhem-pe.*
Practicable, to be	*thup-pa.*
Practice (custom)	*luk-so.*
Practise, to	*jang-wa.*
Praise, s	*to-tra.*
Praise, to	*to-ra tang-wa.*
Pray, to (request)	*shu-wa.*
Prayer (extempore)	*mo-lam.*
Prayer (written)	*khan-don.*
Prayer-wheel	*ma-ni; la-kor.*
Preach, to	*chho she-pa.*
Precede, to	*ngen-la dro-wa.*
Preceding	*ngon-kyi; tang-po.*
Precious	*tsa-chhem-po.*
Precipice	*yang.*
Precipitate (rash)	*kha-me mik-me.*
Precise	*thrik-thrik; ten-ten.*
Precisely	*rang.*

Preclude, to	*kak-pa.*
Predict, to	*ngon-she she-pa.*
Prediction	*lung-ten.*
Prefix, s	*ngon-ju.*
Pregnant, to be	*pu-gu kye-gyu yo-pa.*
Prejudice	*nam-to.*
Prepare, to	*tra-dri che-pa.*
Prerogative	*thop-thang.*
Presage, s	*tem dre.*
Presence of, in the	*dun-la.*
Present, at	*tan-da.*
Present, to	*ter-wa.*
Present, to be	*de yo-pa.*
Present, s. (alms to poor)	*jim-pa.*
Presently (in a few minutes)	*hrip-tsa-chi; gyok-po.*
Preserve, to (keep care of)	*nyar-wa.*
Press, to (insist)	*u-tshu che-pa.*
Press, to (physically)	*nem-pa.*
Pressing (work)	*thre-thre che go-ya.*
Pretend, to	*kyo she-pa.*
Pretty (of things)	*nying-je-po.*
Pretty (of woman)	*tshar-po; dze-po.*
Prevail over, to (overcome)	*gyo-wa; la khe-pa.*

Prevent, to   *kak-pa.*

Previous   *ngon-kyi; tang-po.*

Previously   *ngen-ma; ngen-la.*

Price   *kong; ring.*

Prick, to   *tsuk-pa.*

Pride   *nyam; dza-kho.*

Priest   *la-ma.*

Prince   *gye-se.*

Princess   *gye-po se-mo.*

Principal   *chhe-sho.*

Principally   *phe-chher.*

Principle (origin)   *chung-tang.*

Print, to   *par-gyap-pa.*

Printed matter   *par-ma.*

Printer   *par-pa.*

Printing-office   *par-khang.*

Prior, adj.   *ngon-kyi; tang-po.*

Prison   *tson-khang.*

Prisoner   *tsom-pa.*

Private   *sang-wa.*

Privately   *sang-wa che-ne.*

Privilege (right)   *thop-thang.*

Prize   *so-re.*

Probably   *chik-che-na.*

Probationer (in monastery)
   en-chhung.

Proceed, to   *dro-wa; chhim-pa.*

Proclaim, to   *drok-pa.*

Proclamation (of government)
   ka-gya.

Procrastinating   *nya-si-gu-si.*

Procreate, to   *kye-pa.*

Procure, to   *jor-wa; thop-pa.*

Prodigal (profuse)   *be-po; dzak-to.*

Prodigious   *chhe-thak-chho.*

Prodigy   *yam-tshen.*

Produce, to (bring)
   khyer-yong-wa.

Productive (of soil)   *lu-chhu dzom-po.*

Profane   *chho-sem me-pa.*

Profession   *le-ka.*

Professor   *khem-po.*

Profit   *khep-sang.*

Profitable, to be   *phen-thok-pa.*

Profound (deep)   *ting-ring-po.*

Profuse   *be-po; dzak-to.*

Progeny   *pu-gu.*

Prognostication   *lung ten.*

Prohobit, to   *kak.pa.*

Prolific (of soil)   *lu-chhu dzom-po.*

Promiment (eminent)   *ke-tra chhem-po.*

Promise, to   *khe-lang-wa.*

Promoted, to be *ko-ne phar-wa.*

Promptly *gyok-po.*

Promulgate, to *drok-pa.*

Pronounciation *lap-tang; sho tang.*

Proof *ta.*

Prop, s *ka-kyor.*

Prop, to *kyor-wa.*

Proper (befitting) *o-po.*

Property (in land) *sa-chha.*

Prophecy *lung-ten.*

Prophesy, to *ngon-she she-pa.*

Propitious *tem-dre yak-po.*

Proportion *tsho.*

Proprietor *dak-po.*

Prosperity (good fortune) *so-de; so-nam.*

Prosperous *yang-chhem-po.*

Prostitute *chhe-ma; shang-tshong-ma.*

Prostrate onself, to *chha-tshe-wa.*

Protect, to *sung-wa.*

Protector *kyam-gon.*

Protectorate (over a country) *kyap-khong.*

Proud *nyam-chhem-po; dza-kho chhem-po.*

Prove, to (a case) *ra-thro-pa.*

Prove, to (test) *tsho ta-wa.*

Proverb *tam-pe.*

Provide, to *drup-pa.*

Province *shing-chhen; khu.*

Provisions *kha-la; to.*

Provisions for journey *lam-chhe.*

Provoke, to (annoy) *khong-thro lang-wa.*

Proximity *nye-khor.*

Proxy *tshap.*

Prudence (wisdom) *lo-tro.*

Prudent *khe-po.*

Puddle (small pool) *chhu-khyil.*

Puff (pastry) *mo-mo.*

Pull, to *them-pa.*

Pull, to (of horses) *ngar-po che-pa.*

Pulse (of body) *tsa.*

Punctually *ten-ten che-ne; ma-chhuk-pa che-ne*

Pungent *kha-tsha-po.*

Punish to (by fine) *nye-pa tang-wa.*

Punish, to (by beating) *thrim tang-wa.*

Punishment (by beating) *thrim.*

Punishment (by fine) *nye-pa; chhe-pa.*

Pupil *lap-thru.*

Puppy *a-yo.*

Purchase, to *nyo-wa.*

Pure *tsang-ma.*

Purgative *dri-men; she-men.*

Purge, to *drim-pa; she-wa.*

Purified *tak-po.*

Purple *gun-drum-do.*

Purport *ton-ta.*

Purpose, to *sem-la sam-pa.*

Purpose, s *ton-ta.*

Purr, to *nguk-pa gyap-pa.*

Purse *ba-khu.*

Pursue, to *shuk-de chhim pa.*

Pus *na.*

Push, to *be-kya tang-wa.*

Pustule *thor-pa.*

Put in order, to *drik-pa.*

Put in, to *chuk-pa.*

Put off, to (defer) *pa-su shak-pa.*

Put off, to (divest) *pi-pa.*

Put on, to (clothes) *kom-pa.*

Put, to (place) *shak-pa.*

Putrefy, to *ru-dro-wa.*

Putrid, to be *ru-wa.*

Puzzled, to be *go-thom-pa.*

Q

Quaint *yam-tshen-po; khye-tsha-po.*

Quake, to (shudder) *dar-wa.*

Qualified *o-po.*

Quality *ya-nye; pu-kha.*

Quarrel *gyam-dre.*

Quarrei, to *gyam-dre gyap-pa.*

Quarrel, to pick a *nye-ko-wa.*

Quarrelsome *ru-ngar-po.*

Queen *gye-mo.*

Queer *khye-tsha-po.*

Query, to(question) *tri-wa.*

Question, to *tri-wa.*

Queue (pil-tail) *chang-lo.*

Quick (active) *hur-po.*

Quick (irritable) *ru-ngar-po.*

Quick (living) *som-po.*

Quick (rapid) *gyok-po.*

Quick-silver *ngu-chhu.*

Quickly (rapidly) *gyok-po.*

Quiet (of persons) *kha nyung-nyung.*

Quiet (of places) *kha-ku sim-po.*

Quill-pen *dro-nyu.*

Quilt *nye-sen.*

Quit, to (a country, etc.) *sha-ne yong-wa.*

Quit, to (depart) *thom-pa; chhim-pa.*

Quite (used negatively) *be-te; khyon-ne.*

Quite so! *ta-ka-rang-re.*

Quiver, s *da-tong.*

Quiver, to (of animate things) *dar-wa.*

Quiver, to (of inanimate things) *thruk-pa.*

Quota *ke-la.*

R

Rabbit *ri-kong.*

Rabid *nyom-pa.*

Rabid, to be *nyo-wa.*

Race (tribe) *mi-gyu; ri gyu.*

Race, foot *mi-gyu.*

Racite, to *chho lok-pa.*

Rackless *kha-me mik-me.*

Radiance *si-ji; o.*

Radiant *si-ji chhem-po; chhem-po.*

Radish *la-phu.*

Rafter *cham.*

Rag *a-chho.*

Rage *tshik-pa; khong-thro.*

Ragged *tsap-re.*

Railing (fence) *ra-wa.*

Raiment *tu-lo.*

Raiment, hon. *nam-sa.*

Rain *chhar-pa.*

Rain heavily, to *chhar-pa she-tra gyap-pa.*

Rain, light shower of *tring-chhar.*

Rain, to *chhar-pa tang-wa.*

Rainbow *ja.*

Raise up, to *yar-kyak-pa : yar-lem-pa.*

Raisin *gun-drum ka-po.*

Rake *gya-sep.*

Ram *luk-pho.*

Ramble, to *chham-chham che-pa.*

Ramrod of gun *sim-bi.*

Rancid *kha-tsup-po.*

Rancour *no-sem.*

Range, to *chham-chham la dro-wa.*

Rank (degree) *ko-sa; ko-ne; rim-pa.*

Ransack, to *chak-pa gyap-pa.*

Ransom (for killing a man) *tong.*

Ransom, to *lu-wa.*

Rap, to *tak-tak tang-wa.*

Rap, s. (on door, etc.) *tak-tak.*

Rapacious *do-pa chhem-po; ham-pa tsha-po.*

Rapacity *ham-pa.*

Rapid *gyok-po.*

Rapid, hon. *tso-po.*

Rare *kom-po.*

Rascal *ten-shi; dzap-chhen.*

Rase, to *shik-pa.*

Rash, adj. *kha-me mik-me.*

Rat *tsi-tsi.*

Rate (price) *kong.*

Rate (tax) *thre; bap.*

Ratify, to (confirm) *ten-den che-pa.*

Rattle, to, v.t. *trok-tro tang-wa.*

Ravage, to (rob) *chak-pa gyap-pa.*

Raven *pho-ro.*

Ravine *rong.*

Raw (uncooked) *jem-pa.*

Ray *o-ser.*

Raze, to *shik-pa.*

Razor *tra-tri.*

Reach, to (arrive at) *lep-pa.*

Reach, to (by stretching hand etc.) *nyop-pa.*

Read, to *lok-pa.*

Ready *tra-dri.*

Ready, to make *tra-dri che-pa.*

Real *ngo-tho; ngo-ne.*

Realise, to (obtain) *jor-wa; thop-pa.*

Realise, to (understand) *she-pa; ha-ko-wa.*

Really *nge-par; ngo-ne trang-ne.*

Realm (kingdom) *gye-si.*

Reap, to *nga-wa.*

Reaper *nga-khen.*

Rear, in the *gyap-la.*

Reason (mind) *lo; sem.*

Reason (purpose) *ton-ta.*

Reason, to (argue) *tse gyap-pa.*

Rebel, to *de-thruk-pa.*

Rebellion *de-thru.*

Rebuke, to *she-she tang-wa.*

Rebuke, s. *she-she.*

Recede, to (retreat) *chhi-lo gyap-pa.*

Receipt *dzin.*

Receive, to *jor-wa; thop-pa.*

Recent *sa-pa.*

Recently *kha-sang-ne.*

Reckon, to *tsi-gyap-pa.*

Recline, to *nye-ne de-pa.*

Recluse   *gom-chhen.*

Recognise, to (a person)   *ngo-shem-pa.*

Recollect, to   *tren-so-wa.*

Recollection   *trem-pa.*

Reconciliation   *nang-dri.*

Record   *tho.*

Recover, to (health)   *trak-pa.*

Recover, to(find)   *nye-pa.*

Rectify   *shu-ta che-pa.*

Red   *mar-po.*

Reed   *nyung-ma.*

Refuge   *kyam-ne.*

Refuse, to (a request)   *mi....nyem-pa.*

Region   *lung-pa.*

Reject, to   *pang-wa.*

Relate, to   *she-pa.*

Relation   *nye-wa.*

Relative, s   *nye-wa.*

Release, to   *thar-ra che-pa;*
tang-wa.

Released, to be   *thar-wa.*

Reliable   *lo khe-wa.*

Reliance   *lo-te.*

Relief (help)   *ro.*

Religion   *chho.*

Religious   *chho-sem chhem-po.*

Rely on , to   *lo kel-wa.*

Remain, to   *de-pa.*

Remainder   *hla-ma.*

Remarkable   *khye-tsha-po.*

Remember, to   *tren-so-wa.*

Remembrance   *trem-pa.*

Remind, to   *tren-so tang-wa.*

Reminder   *tren-so.*

Remorse (regret)   *gye-pa.*

Remorseless, to be (merciless)
nying-je me-pa.

Remote   *tha-ring-po.*

Remove, to   *pha shi-pa.*

Remove, to (take off)   *pi-pa.*

Remuneration   *ngem-pa.*

Rend, to   *shak-pa.*

Renounce, to   *pang-wa.*

Renown   *ke-tra.*

Renowned   *ming chhem-po.*

Rent   *se-ka.*

Rent of a house   *khang-la.*

Rent, to (house)   *khang-la*
che-ne de-pa.

Repair, to   *so-kyor che-pa.*

Repair, to (a house)   *shik-so*
che-pa.

Repast   *kha-la; to.*

Repay, to   *khin-tshap tre-pa.*

Repeat, to (recite) *chho-lok-pa.*

Repent, to *gyo-pa kye-pa.*

Repentance *gyo-pa.*

Reply to a letter, s. *yik-len.*

Reply, to *len gyap-pa.*

Reply, to(letter) *yik-len tang-wa.*

Reply, s. *len.*

Report (rumour) *ke-chha; tam.*

Report, to *nyen-shu tang-wa.*

Report, to (after investigation) *thra-ma phu-wa.*

Repository *pang-dzo.*

Representative *tshap; thu-mi.*

Reprimand, s. *she-she.*

Reprimand, to *she-she tang-wa.*

Reproduce, to (copy) *pe-shu-wa.*

Reproduce, to (imitate) *mik-dren che-pa.*

Reprove, to *she-she tang-wa.*

Repulsive *kyuk-tro-po.*

Reputable *ya-rap.*

Reputation (fame) *ke-tra.*

Repute, s. *ke-tra.*

Repute, s.hon. *nyen-tra.*

Request, s. *shu-wa.*

Request, to *shu-wa.*

Require, to *go-pa.*

Requisite *go-pa.*

Requite, to (revenge) *dra-len lok-pa.*

Rescue, to *kyap-pa; kyong-wa.*

Resent, to *tsher-wa.*

Resentment *tshik-pa; khong-thro.*

Resentment, to cause *khong-thro lang-wa.*

Reside, to *de-pa.*

Residence (house) *khang-pa; nang; do-sa*

Resident *do-khen.*

Residue *hla-ma.*

Resistless, to be *kak....mi-thup-pa*

Resolute *tem-po.*

Resolve, to (decide) *tha-che-pa.*

Resoning *tso-pa.*

Respect (reverence) *nyen-kur.*

Respect to, with *ton-la; kor-la.*

Respect, to *nyen-kur che-pa.*

Respectable (socially) *ya-rap.*

Respectful language *she-sa.*

Respecting (concerning) *ton-la; kor-la.*

Respiration *u.*

Resplendence *si-ji.*

Resplendent *si-ji chhem-po; o chhem-po.*

Respond, to *len gyan-pa.*

Responsibility   *kha; gen.*

Responsible, to become   *khe-khyak-pa.*

Rest (for Tibetan gun)   *men-de ru.*

Rest, to   *nge-so-wa.*

Rest, to (elbows on table, etc.)
              bo-nye gyap-pa.

Rest, to (lie down)   *nye-de-pa.*

Rest, to (lean back)   *gyam-nye gyap-pa.*

Rest, to (lean back), hon.   *ku-nye kyom-pa.*

Restaurant   *sa-khang.*

Restaurant   *za-khang.*

Restaurant   *za-khang.*

Restrain, to   *kak-pa.*

Result   *nying-po.*

Ret, to   *rul-wa.*

Retain, to   *shak-pa.*

Retaliate, to   *dra-len lok-pa.*

Retaliation   *dra-len.*

Retard to (obstruct)   *kak-pa.*

Retinue   *khor-yo.*

Retire, to (retreat)   *chhi-lo gyap-pa.*

Retreat, s. (shelter)   *kyam-ne.*

Retreat, to   *chhi-lo gyap-pa.*

Return, to   *lok-pa.*

Return, to, v.t.   *tsi tre-pa.*

Revenge, s.   *dra-len.*

Revenge, to   *dra-len lok-pa.*

Revenue   *thre-ngu.*

Revenue, government   *shung-gi bap.*

Reverence, to   *ngen-kur che-pa.*

Reverence, s.   *nyen-kur.*

Reverend (title)   *je-tsun.*

Reverse, to   *nyen-kur che-pa.*

Reverse, to (turn back to front)
              kha-chho lok-pa.

Reverse, to (turn up-side down)
              go-shu lok-pa; a-lo gyap-pa.

Revile, to   *me-ra tang-wa.*

Revise, to   *shu-ta tang-wa.*

Revision   *shu-ta.*

Revolt, s.   *de-thru.*

Revolt, to   *de-thruk-pa.*

Revolting (disgusting)   *kyuk-tro-po.*

Revolve, to   *khor-wa.*

Reward   *ngem-pa.*

Reward, to   *ngem-pa ter-wa.*

Rheumatism   *bam.*

Rhinoceros   *se-ru.*

Rhododendron   *ta-ma-shing.*

Rhubarb   *chhu-chhu.*

Rib   *tsi-ma.*

Ribbon   *hle-ma.*

Rice   *dre.*

Rich (fertile)   *lu-chhu dzom-po.*

Rich (wealthy)   *chhuk-po;*
cha-la chhem-po.

Ride, to   *shom-pa.*

Ridge   *gang.*

Ridiculous   *ton-me.*

Riding horse   *shon-ta.*

Riding mule   *shon-tre.*

Riding pony   *shon-ta.*

Rifle   *men-da.*

Rift   *se-ka.*

Right ! (very well)   *la-si;*
la-la-si.

Right (not left)   *ye.*

Right (not wrong)   *tak-po.*

Right (privilege)   *thop-thang.*

Right now   *dha-ta-rang.*

Right, to be   *drik-pa.*

Righteous   *trang-po.*

Rigid   *thrak-po.*

Rind   *pak-pa.*

Rinderpest   *yor.*

Ring   *tshi-kho.*

Ring (circle)   *a-long.*

Ring (for thumb)   *tre-kho.*

Ring, to (bell)   *trol-wa.*

Ringleader   *te-po; mi-che*
go-che che-khen.

Rinse, to   *she-she tang-wa.*

Ripen, to   *mim-pa.*

Rise, to (get up)   *lang-wa.*

Rise, to (of sun)   *shar-wa.*

Risk   *nyen-kha.*

Risky   *nyen-kha chhem-po.*

Rite, religious   *chho-lu.*

Rival   *khap-the.*

River   *tsang-chhu.*

Road   *lang-ka.*

Road, main   *gya-lam.*

Roam, to   *chham-chham che-pa.*

Roar, to (wild beasts)   *ngar-ke*
gyap-pa.

Roast, to   *ngo-pa.*

Rob, to (by stealth)   *ku-ma*
ku-wa.

Robber (by stealth)   *ku-ma.*

Robe   *tu-lo.*

Robust   *she chhem-po.*

Rock   *tra.*

Rockoning   *tsi.*

Rod   *khar-gyu.*

Roe (of fish)   *nye-go-nga.*

Rogue   *ten-shi; dzap-chhen.*

Roll (of woollen cloth)   *pup.*

Roll, to   *dril-wa.*

Roof   *tho-kha.*

96

Rook	*kha-ta.*	Ruffian	*dzap-chhen.*
Room (in house)	*khang-mi.*	Rug (bedding)	*nye-sen.*
Room (space)	*sa-chha.*	Rugged	*tsup-po.*
Root	*tsa-wa.*	Ruin, to	*me-pa so-wa.*
Rope	*thak-pa.*	Rule (government)	*shung; shung-tho.*
Rosary	*thrang-nga.*		
Rose	*se-we me-to.*	Rule (law)	*thrim.*
Rosin	*thang-chhu.*	Rule (maxim)	*tam-pe.*
Rotten	*ru-pa.*	Rule a country, to (secular rule) *gye-si nang-wa.*	
Rough	*tsup-po; tsing-po.*	Rule, as a (usually)	*nam-gyun.*
Round (like a disc)	*go-gor.*	Rule, to (decide)	*tha-che-pa.*
Rouse, to (from sleep)	*nyi se-pa.*	Rule, to (govern)	*wang che-pa.*
Route	*lang-ka.*	Ruler (king)	*gye-po.*
Route (high way)	*gya-lam.*	Rumour	*ke-chha; tam.*
Rove, to	*chham-chham che-pa.*	Rump (anus)	*kup.*
Row (line)	*tre.*	Run away, to (flee)	*po-chhim-pa.*
Row (noise)	*u-dra.*	Run, to	*gyuk-pa.*
Row, to (boat)	*kya-gyap-pa.*	Rupee	*gor-mo.*
Royal	*gye-po.*	Rust	*tsa.*
Rub out, to (erase)	*sup-pa.*	Rut (furrow)	*rol.*
Rub, to	*phu-phu che-pa.*	Ruthless, to be	*nying-je me-pa.*
Rubber	*gyi.*		
Rubbish (refuse)	*ke-nyi; chha-nyi.*		
Ruby	*pe-ma ra-ga.*	Sabbath	*nge-so-we nyi-ma.*
Rudder	*kyam-ju.*	Sabre	*sho-lang.*
Rude (impolite)	*jing-pa bom-po; kyong-po.*	Sack (small)	*phe-ko.*

S

Sacred	*tam-pa; chhon-den.*	Salute, to	*chham-bu shu-wa.*
Sacrifice	*chho-pa.*	Salvation	*thar-pa.*
Sacrifice, to	*chho-pa phu-wa.*	Same	*chik-pa.*
Sad, to be	*sem-kyo-wa; sem-duk-pa.*	Sample	*pe; pu-tshe.*
Saddle	*ga; te-ga.*	Sanctify, to (consecrate)	*rap-ne che-pa.*
Saddle, to	*te-ga gyap-pa.*	Sanction	*ton-min.*
Saddle, pack	*khe-ga.*	Sand	*chhe-ma.*
Saddle-cloth	*ma-tren.*	Sand-grouse	*kang-ka-ling.*
Saddle-girth	*lo.*	Sandal	*tre-pa.*
Saddle-lag	*ta-dro.*	Sandal-wood	*lsen-ten.*
Safe (steadfast)	*tem-po.*	Sanskrit	*nga-ke.*
Safflower (saffron)	*kur-kum.*	Sap	*chhu.*
Saffron	*kha-che sha-ka-ma.*	Sapient	*yon-ten chhem-po.*
Sagacious	*rik-pa chhem-po.*	Sapphire	*in-tra-m-la.*
Sagacity	*rik-pa.*	Sash	*ke-ra.*
Sailor	*nyem-pa.*	Satan	*du.*
Saint, Buddhist	*chang-chhup sem-pa.*	Satin (cloth)	*sup.*
Saintly	*tam-pa; chhon-den.*	Satisfied, to be	*do-pa kang-wa.*
Sake of, for the	*ton-la.*	Satisfied, to be(with food)	*drang-wa.*
Salad	*dang-tshel.*	Saturday	*sa-pem-pa.*
Salammoniac	*gya-tsha.*	Saturday	*za pen-pa.*
Salary	*pho.*	Sauce	*sha-khv*
Salesman	*tshong-pa.*	Saucepan	*tshe-lang*
Saliva	*kha-chhu.*	Saucer	*tra-kya.*
Salt	*tsha.*	Saucy (rude)	*jing-pa bom-po; kyong-po.*
Saltpetre	*se-tsha.*		

Saunter, to (linger) *gor-wa.*

Sausage *gyu-ma.*

Savage, s. (barbarian) *la-lo.*

Save, to (money) *sak-pa.*

Save, to (rescue) *kyap-pa.*

Saviour *kyam-gon.*

Savour *tro.*

Savoury *shim-po.*

Saw (cutting instrument) *so-le.*

Saw (proverb) *tam-pe.*

Saw. to *so-le gyap-pa.*

Say, to *lap-pa; se-wa.*

Saying *ke-chha.*

Scab *ma-kho.*

Scabbard *shup.*

Scalded, to be *chhu-kho-me tshik-pa.*

Scales a pair of *nya-ga.*

Scamp *ten-shi; dzap-chhen.*

Scan, to (look at) *ta-wa.*

Scanty *nyung-nyung.*

Scar *ma-je.*

Scarce *kom-po.*

Scare, to *she-tra lang-wa.*

Scared, to be *she-pa.*

Scarlet *ma-po.*

Scart, complimentary, best *nang-dzo.*

Scart, complimentary *kha-ta.*

Scatter, to (strew) *tor-wa.*

Scent, s. *tri-ma.*

Sceptre (thunder bolt) *dor-je.*

Schedule *sur-tho.*

Scholar (pupil) *lap-thru.*

Scholarly (learned) *yon-ten chhem-po.*

School *lap-tra.*

School-master *ge-gen.*

Science (knowledge) *she-cha.*

Science (skill) *rik-pa.*

Scissors *chem-tse.*

Scoff, to *kya-kya che-ne lap-pa.*

Scold, to *she-she tang-wa.*

Scoop, s. *kyo.*

Scoop, to *kyo-kyi tom-pa.*

Scope (intention) *ton-ta.*

Score (twenty) *nyi-shu.*

Scorn, to *kya-kya che-ne lap-pa.*

Scorpion *dik-pa ra-dza.*

Scoundral *ten-shi; dzap-chhen.*

Scourge, to *te-cha shu-wa.*

Scraggy (of persons & animals) *sha kam-po.*

Scrap *tum-pu.*

Scrape off, to	*shu-shu che-pa.*
Scrape, to	*tre-tre tang-wa.*
Scratch, to	*bar-she gyap-pa.*
Scream, to	*ke-gyap-pa.*
Screen	*yo-la.*
Scriptures	*sung-rap.*
Scroll	*shuk-ku chhak-pa.*
Scruple	*the-tshom.*
Sea	*gyam-tsho.*
Seal	*tam-thru; the-tse.*
Sealing-wax	*la-chha.*
Seam	*tshem-pu.*
Seamail	*tsho-dag.*
Search, to	*tshik-pa.*
Search, to	*tshel-wa.*
Season	*nam-tu.*
Seat	*kup-kya; thri-u-shing.*
Secluded place	*en-ne.*
Second	*nyi-pa.*
Second (time)	*kar-cha.*
Secondly	*nyi-pa.*
Secret	*sang-wa.*
Secretary	*trung-yi dre-pa.*
Secretary, Chief	*trung-yi chhem-mo-wa.*
Secrete, to	*be-pa.*
Sect (religious)	*chho-lu.*
Secular	*jik-tem-pa.*
Secure (steadfast)	*tem-po.*
Security (bail)	*khe-khya.*
Security, to give	*khe-khya che-pa.*
Sedan-chair	*gyo-chang.*
Sediment	*nyi.*
Seduce, to	*lu-wa.*
See, to	*thong-wa.*
Seek, to	*tshel-wa.*
Seemingly (probably)	*yim-pa-dra.*
Seemly (becoming)	*o-po.*
Seize, to	*sim-pa.*
Select, to	*dam-pa.*
Self	*rang.*
Selfish	*rang-do tsha-po.*
Selfishness	*rang-do*
Sell, to	*tshong-wa.*
Send, to	*tang-wa.*
Senior	*gem-pa.*
Sense (opinion)	*sam-pa.*
Sense (purport)	*ton-ta.*
Sense (understanding)	*lo-tro.*
Senseless (nonsensical)	*ton-me.*
Sensible (intelligent)	*rik-pa yak-po.*
Sentence s. (in a book)	*shok-lo.*

Sentence, to (fine)   *nye-pa tang-wa.*

Sentence, to (punish)   *thrim tang-wa.*

Sentiment (opinion)   *sam-pa.*

Sentinel   *so-pa.*

Separate, to   *yen chhe-wa.*

Separately   *kha-kha che-ne.*

Sepoy   *ma-mi.*

September   *chin-dha gu-pa.*

Sepulchre   *ro be-sa.*

Series   *rim-pa.*

Serpent   *dru.*

Serpent-demon   *lu.*

Servant   *yok-po.*

Servant, female   *she-ta-ma.*

Serve, to   *yo che-pa.*

Service, religious   *chho-ga; ku-rim.*

Serviceable, to be   *phen-thok-pa.*

Sesamum   *til.*

Set out, to (depart)   *thom-pa.*

Set right to (adjust)   *drik-pa.*

Set right, to (adjust) hon.   *drik-ka nang-wa.*

Set, to (place)   *shak-pa.*

Set, to (of the sun)   *ge-pa.*

Settle (to (decide)   *tha che-pa.*

Settle to (arrange)   *drik-pa.*

Settle, to (a lawsuit out of court)   *dum tang-wa.*

Seven   *dhun.*

Seventeen   *chup-dun.*

Seventeenth   *chup-dun-pa.*

Seventh   *dun-pa.*

Seventieth   *dun-chu-pa.*

Seventy   *dun-chu.*

Sever, to (cut)   *che-pa.*

Several   *ga-chhen.*

Severally   *so-so che-ne.*

Severe (harsh, of human beings)   *kyong-po.*

Severe (of gods)   *trak-po.*

Severe (strict)   *tam-po; tsem-po.*

Sew, to   *tshem-pa; tshem-pu gyap-pa.*

Sew, to (together)   *drel-wa.*

Shackles (for hands)   *lak-cha.*

Shade   *sil-trip.*

Shadow   *tri-ma.*

Shaggy   *tsup-po.*

Shake, to (of brige etc.)   *dem-dem che-pa.*

Shake, to (of human being) hon   *kun-dar kyom-pa.*

Shake, to v.i.   *thruk-pa.*

Shake, to v.t. *gu-gu tang-wa;*
            truk-truk che-pa.

Shallow, to be   *ting-ring-po*
            me-pa.

Sham (false)   *dzu-ma.*

Sham illness, to   *na-dzu tap-pa.*

Sham, to   *kyo she-pa.*

Shame   *nge-tsha.*

Shame, to feel   *ngo-tsha-wa.*

Shamefaced   *ngo-tsha-po.*

Shameful   *ngo-tsha-po.*

Shameless, to be   *ngo-tsha me-pa.*

Shape, n.   *sop-ta,* .

Share   *ke-la.*

Share, to   *go-pa; gop-sha*
            gyap-pa.

Share, to, hon.   *go-pa nang-wa;*
            gop-sha kyom-pa.

Sharp (not blunt)   *no-po.*

Sharpen, to (by blacksmith)
            khan-don che-pa.

Sharpen, to   *dar-wa.*

Shatter, to   *hru-hru tang-wa.*

Shave, to   *tra shar-wa.*

Shaved head (as a monk) *go-ri-ri.*

Shawl (of lamas)   *sen.*

She   *mo.*

Sheaf   *chhak-pa.*

Shear, to   *pe pak-pa.*

Shear, to hon.   *pe pak-ka*
            nang-wa.

Sheep   *lu.*

Sheep, flock of   *luk-khyu.*

Sheep-skin   *luk-pa.*

Sheet of paper   *shu-ku.*

Shelf   *pang-thri; pang-ka.*

Shell   *drom-pu.*

Shell, conch   *tung.*

Shelter (refuge)   *kyam-ne.*

Shepherd   *luk-dzi.*

Shield   *phup.*

Shift, to (move)   *po-wa.*

Shin, shiu-bone   *ngar-tung.*

Shine (brightness)   *o.*

Shine, to   *o gyap-pa.*

Shine, to (of the sun)   *shar-wa.*

Ship   *tru.*

Shirt   *to-thung.*

Shiver, to   *dar-wa.*

Shoe   *hlam.*

Shoe (European style)   *ju-ta.*

Shoe-maker   *hlam-so.*

Shook   *ngam-tra.*

Shoot, to (with gun, etc.) *gyap-pa.*

Shop   *tshong-khang.*

Shore   *dram.*

Short   *thung-thung.*

Short man   *te-po.*

Short-cut (road)   *gyo-lam.resume*

Shorten, to (abbreviate)   *du-pa;*
dum-dum che-pa.

Shortly (soon)   *hrip-tsa-chi-la.*

Shoulder   *pung-pa.*

Shout, to   *ke-gyap-pa.*

Shovel   *ja-ma.*

Show   *te-mo.*

Show off, to (in dress)   *tang-do*
che-pa.

Show, to   *tem-pa.*

Shower of rain, light   *tring-chhar.*

Shrewd   *chang-po.*

Shrine   *hla-khang.*

Shrink, to (of cloth, etc.)
khum-pa.

Shrivel, to   *khum-pa.*

Shrub   *shing-dong-chung-chung.*

Shudder, to   *dar-wa.*

Shun, to (persons)   *yo-wa;*
sur-ne dro-wa.

Shun, to (things)   *yuk-shak-pa;*
pang-wa.

Shut the mouth, to   *kha tsum-pa.*

Shut up ! (keep quiet)   *kha-kha-*
do; kha-tsum.

Shut, to (door)   *gyap-pa.*

Shutter   *go-pang.*

Shuttle-cock   *the-be.*

Shy, to (of horses)   *drok-pa.*

Shy, to be (bashful)   *ngo-tsha-wa.*

Sick, to be   *na-wa.*

Sickle   *sor-ra.*

Sickness   *na-tsha.*

Side (of the body)   *sur.*

Side of, the far   *phar-chho.*

Side of, the near   *tshur-chho.*

Side of, at the   *tsa-la.*

Sides, on all   *phen-tshun.*

Sift, to   *tsak-pa.*

Sigh   *u-ring.*

Sigh, to   *u-ring tang-wa.*

Sight (of a gun)   *so-khung.*

Sightless   *long-nga.*

Sign (mark)   *ta.*

Signal   *lak-da.*

Signature   *lak-ta.*

Significant (important)   *nen-kha*
chhem-po; ke chhem-po

Signification   *ton-ta.*

Sikkim   *dren-jong.*

Silent, to be   *kha-kha de-pa.*

Silk   *du-tsi.*

Silly (weak in intellect)   *kuk-pa;*
lem-pa.

Silver **ngul-dhog.**

Silver (metal) **ngu'e.**

Silversmith **ngu so-wa.**

Simple (easy) **le-la-po.**

Simpleton **kuk-pa; lem-pa.**

Simply (merely) **chik-ko.**

Simulate, to **kyo she-pa.**

Sin **dik-pa.**

Sin, to **dik-pa sak-pa.**

Since (afterwards) **shu-la; je-la.**

Sincere **trang-po.**

Sincerely **ngo-ne trang-ne.**

Sinew **gyu-pa.**

Sinful **ngem-po.**

Sing, to (hymns) **gur-ma lem-pa.**

Sing, to **she tang-wa.**

Single (individual) **re-re.**

Single (separate) **chik-po.**

Singly **re-re ce-ne.**

Sink, to (of things) **sak-pa.**

Sink, to (of persons) **thim-pa.**

Sinner **dik-chen.**

Sinuous **kyo-kyo.**

Sip, to **tok-tso tok-tso thung-wa.**

Sir **ku-she.**

Sister (general term) **pun-kya.**

Sister, elder **a-chhe.**

Sister, young **pun-kya chhung-na.**

Sister-in-law (brother's wife) **pun-kya ki kyi-men.**

Sister-in-law (husband's sister) **khyo-ge pun-kya.**

Sister-in-law (wife's sister) **kyi-men-kyi pun-kya.**

Sit cross-legged, to **kyi-trung che-ne de-pa.**

Sit, to **de-pa.**

Site **sa-chha.**

Situation (locality) **sa-chha.**

Six **dug.**

Sixteen **chu-truk.**

Sixteenth **chu-truk-pa.**

Sixth **truk-pa.**

Sixtieth **truk-chu-pa.**

Sixty **dug-chu.**

Size **chhe-chhung.**

Skeleton **ru-trang.**

Sketch **ri-mo.**

Sketch, to **ri-mo tri-pa.**

Skilful **khe-po.**

Skill **rik-pa.**

Skin **pag-pa.**

Skin, to **pak-pa shu-wa.**

Skinny (of persons and animals)
    sha kam-po.

Skull   *kab-li.*

Skull-drum   *thon-tam.*

Sky   *nam; nam-kha.*

Slack (languid)   *nya-re nyo-re.*

Slacken, to   *hlo-hlo tang-wa.*

Slander, to   *me-ra tang-wa.*

Slander. s.   *me-ra.*

Slap, to   *shu-wa.*

Slate, (for writing)   *yam-pa.*

Slaughter, to   *se-pa.*

Slave   *tshe-yo.*

Slay, to   *se-pa.*

Sleep, s.   *nyi.*

Sleep, to   *nye de-pa.*

Sleep, to go to   *nyi khuk-pa.*

Sleeping draught   *shi-men.*

Sleeping pill   *nyee-men.*

Sleepy, to be   *nyi-tso gyap-pa.*

Sleeve   *phu-tung.*

Slender   *thra-po.*

Slice   *tra-po.*

Slice, to   *tup-pa.*

Slight, adj.(thin)   *sha kam-po.*

Sling (for stone)   *gu-do.*

Slip, to, v.i.   *dre-ta shor-wo.*

Slit (fissure)   *ser-ka.*

Slit, to be (cloth)   *re-wa.*

Slope (upward)   *kyen.*

Slothful   *nyop-po; le-lo chhem-po.*

Slow   *gor-po.*

Slowly   *ka-le ka-le.*

Sluggard   *nyop-po.*

Sluggish (languid)   *nya-re nyo-re.*

Slumber, to   *nyi-tso gyap-pa.*

Sly (artful)   *chang-po.*

Small   *chhung-chhung.*

Small-pox   *hlan-drum.*

Smash, to   *chak-pa.*

Smear, to   *chuk-pa; ku-wa.*

Smell   *tri-ma.*

Smell, to (have odour)   *tri-ma kha-wa.*

Smile, to   *kha tshe-tshe che-pa.*

Smite, to   *shu-wa; dung-wa.*

Smith   *gar-ra.*

Smoke, to (tobacco)   *thung-wa; them-pa.*

Smoke, s.   *tu-wa.*

Smooth   *nyom-po.*

Smother, to   *lo-sup gyap-pa.*

Snake   *dru.*

Snap the finger, to   *sir-kor dap-pa.*

Snare   *nyi.*

Snatch, to   *throk-pa.*

Sneer, to   *kya-kya che-ne lap-pa.*

Sneeze, to   *hap-tri gyap-pa.*

Snore, to   *ngur-pa gyap-pa.*

Snow   *kang.*

Snow, to   *kang gyap-pa.*

Snow, eye-shade for   *mik-ra.*

Snow-avalanche   *kang-ru.*

Snow-blindness   *kang-chhi.*

Snow-cock   *thap-cha kong-mo.*

Snow-leopard   *sa.*

Snow-storm   *kang-tshup.*

Snuff   *na-tha.*

Snuff-box   *na-ru.*

So and so   *den-dre.*

Soak, to   *bang-wa.*

Soap   *yee-tsi.*

Soar, to   *ding-wa.*

Sob, to   *ngu-wa.*

Sober (not drunk), to be   *ra ma si-pa.*

Sock   *o-mo-su.*

Socket of the eye   *mik-khung.*

Sod   *pang.*

Soda   *pu-to.*

Soft   *jam-po.*

Softly   *ka-le ka-le.*

Soil (earth)   *sa.*

Soil, to   *tsok-pa so-wa.*

Sojourn, to   *de-pa.*

Solace, to   *sem-so tang-wa.*

Solder, s.   *ka-ya.*

Soldier   *ma-mi.*

Sole (of foot)   *kang-thi.*

Sole, adj.   *chik-po.*

Solely   *sha-ta.*

Solicit, to   *shu-wa.*

Solid (firm)   *tem-po.*

Solitary   *chik-po.*

Solitary place   *en-ne.*

Sombre, to be, (melancholy)   *sem kyo-nang che-pa.*

Some (a few, e.g. men)   *kha-she.*

Some (a little)   *tok-tsa.*

Something   *ka-re yin-ne chi.*

Sometimes   *tsham-tsham.*

Somnolent, to be   *nyi-cso gyap-pa.*

Son   *pu.*

Son-in-law   *muk-pa.*

Song   *she.*

Song, religious   *gur-ma.*

Soon   *gyok-po.*

Soothsay, to   *ngon-she she-pa.*

Soothsay, to (in a trance)   *lung tem-pa.*

Soothsayer   *tsi-pa.*

Soothsaying   *ngon-she.*

Soothsaying (in a trance)   *lung-ten.*

Sorcerer   *thu-gyap-khen.*

Sorcery   *thu.*

Sordid   *lak-pa tam-po.*

Sore throat, to have a   *ke-na-wa.*

Sore, s.   *ma.*

Sorrow   *du-nge.*

Sorrowful, to be   *sem-kyo-wa; sem-duk-pa.*

Sorry   *gong-dhaa.*

Sorry, to be   *sem-kyo-wa.*

Sort, s. (of things)   *gyu-ta.*

Sort, s. (class of man)   *gyu; ri.*

Sorts, different   *no-tsho.*

Soul   *sem.*

Sound (healthy)   *suk-po de-po.*

Sound (healthy), hon.   *ku-suk sang-po.*

Sound (noise)   *ke.*

Soup   *khu-a.*

Soup (made from meat)   *sha-khu.*

Sour (acid)   *kyur-po.*

Source (of river, etc.)   *chung-tang.*

South   *hlo.*

Sovereign (king)   *gye-po.*

Sow, s.   *pha-mo.*

Sow, to (seed)   *tap-pa.*

Sower   *son gyam-khen.*

Space for, sufficient   *shong-sa.*

Spacious   *ku-yang-po.*

Spade   *ja-ma.*

Span   *tho.*

Spare (thin)   *sha kam-po.*

Spare time (leisure)   *long.*

Spark   *me-tsha.*

Sparkle, to, v.i.   *o gyap-pa.*

Speak, to   *lap-pa.*

Spear   *dung.*

Specially   *khye-par-tu.*

Species (of human beings)   *gyu; ri.*

Species (of things)   *gyu-ta.*

Specimen   *pe.*

Spectacle   *te-mo.*

Spectacles   *mik-sher.*

Spectre (ghost)   *dong-dre; dre.*

Speech   *ke.*

Speechless, to be   *kha-kha de-pa.*

Speed	*tsha-tra.*	Spoon	*thu-maa.*
Speed, to	*gyok-po che-pa.*	Sport, s.	*tse-mo.*
Speedy	*gyok-po.*	Sport, to	*tse-mo tse-wa.*
Spell, to	*jang-lo gyap-pa.*	Spot (stain)	*thik-pa.*
Spelling	*jong-lo.*	Spouse (wife)	*kyi-men.*
Spend wastefully, to	*tor-wa.*	Sprain	*tshig chhu-pa.*
Spice	*men-na.*	Spread, to (mat, etc.)	*ting-wa.*
Spider	*dom.*	Spring	*chee-ka.*
Spider's web	*dom-tha.*	Spring (of water)	*chhu-mi.*
Spike, iron	*chak-phur.*	Spring (season)	*chi-ka.*
Spill, to	*pho-wa.*	Spring, to (jump)	*chhong-pa;*
Spin, to	*khe-wa.*		*chhong-gya gyap-pa.*

Sprinkle, to (e.g. water on ground)   *tor-wa.*

Spindle	*yo-ga.*	Sprite	*dong-dre; dre.*
Spine	*ge-tshi.*	Sprout, to	*kye-wa.*
Spirit (soul)	*sem.*	Spruce (tree)	*se-shing.*
Spirit, evil	*dong-dre; du.*	Spur (of mountain)	*gang.*
Spirited	*hur-po.*	Spy, s.	*so-pa.*
Spiritual	*ge-sem chhem-po.*	Squabble (row)	*gyam-dre.*
Spit, to	*chhi-ma tor-wa.*	Squabble, to	*gyam-dre gyap-pa.*
Spite	*no-sem.*	Squander, to	*tor-wa.*
Spittle	*chhi-ma.*	Square	*trup-shi.*
Splendid	*si-ji chhem-po;*	Squeeze, to	*tsi-wa.*
	yang-dze.	Stab, to	*tsuk-pa.*
Splendour	*si-ji.*	Stable gear	*tap-chhe.*
Splice, to	*thu gyap-pa.*	Stable, adj. (firm)	*tem-po.*
Split, to	*shak-pa.*	Stable, s.	*ta-ra.*
Spoil, to	*me-pa so-wa.*		

Stack, to   *tsik shak-pa.*

Staff   *khar-gyu; gyuk-pa.*

Stag   *sha-pho.*

Stage of a journey   *shak-sa;*
               gya-tshu.

Stagger, to (astonish)   *yom-tshen*
               che-pa.

Stagger, to, v.i.   *khyor-ne dro-wa.*

Stain, s.   *thik-pa.*

Stain, to   *tsok-pa so-wa.*

Stair-case   *ken-tsa.*

Staircase (of stone)   *dop-kya.*

Stake   *nying-pa.*

Stake (wager)   *gyen.*

Stake, to   *gyen shak-pa.*

Stake, to, hon.   *ku-gyen*
               shok-ka nang-wa.

Stalk   *kang.*

Stallion   *sep.*

Stalwart   *she chhem-po.*

Stammering   *kha-di.*

Stamp, s.(seal)   *the-tse; tom-thru.*

Stampede, to   *drok-ne po-pa.*

Stand, to   *lang-ne de-pa.*

Standard (flag)   *tar-cho.*

Star   *kar-ma.*

Stare, to   *mik-dir-ne tar-wa.*

Stare, to, hon.   *chen-dir-ne si-pa.*

Start, to (on a journey)   *dro-wa;*
               chhim-pa.

State (condition)   *ne-tshu.*

Station (rank)   *ko-sa.*

Statue   *kun-da.*

Status quo   *chhap-si ngon-yo.*

Status quo, maintenance of
         chhap-si ngon-yo rang-ja
           shak-gyu.

Stay, to   *de-pa.*

Stay, to (wait)   *gu de-pa.*

Steadfast   *tem-po.*

Steadily   *ten-ten che-ne.*

Steady (resolute)   *tem-po.*

Steal, to   *ku-ma ku-wa; ku-wa.*

Steam   *lang-pa.*

Steath   *shup.*

Steed   *ta.*

Steel   *dhang-chaa.*

Steep   *sar-pa.*

Steep, to   *bang-wa.*

Stem   *dong-po.*

Stench, to   *tri-ma kha-wa.*

Step (pace)   *kom-pa.*

Step, to (move by paces)
            kom-pa gyap-pa.

Step, flight of wooden   *ken-tsa.*

Step-father   *pha-ya.*

Step-mother   *ma-ya.*

Steps, stone   *dop-kya.*

Sterile (of women)   *rap-chhe.*

Stern, adj.   *kyong-po.*

Steward   *chhang-dzo.*

Stick, to (paste) v.t.   *jar-wa.*

Stick, s.   *khar-gyu; gyuk-pa.*

Stiff   *kyong-po.*

Stifle, to   *lo-sup gyap-pa.*

Still, adv.   *ta-rung; tan-do.*

Still, to sit   *kha-kha de-pa.*

Still-birth   *shi-ro kye-pa.*

Sting, to   *so gyap-pa.*

Stingy   *lak-pa tam-po.*

Stink, to   *tri-ma kha-wa.*

Stipend   *la; pho.*

Stir, to (move)   *truk-pa.*

Stir, to, v.i.   *thruk-pa.*

Stir, to (move), v.t., hon.   *truk-ka nang-wa.*

Stirrup   *yop.*

Stirrup-leather   *yop-tha.*

Stitch, to (clothes)   *tshem-pa.*

Stitch, to (together)   *drel-wa.*

Stock (for criminals)   *an-de.*

Stock (of gun)   *gum-shing.*

Stocking   *o-mo-su.*

Stomach   *do-kho.*

Stone   *dho.*

Stool (foot-stool)   *kang-tek.*

Stoop, to   *kuk-ku che-pa.*

Stop raining, to   *chhar-pa chhe-pa.*

Stop, to, v.t.   *kok-pa.*

Stop, to, v.i.   *de-pa.*

Store-house   *dzo; dzo-khang.*

Stork   *trung-trung ka-mo.*

Storm   *lung-tshup.*

Story (legend)   *drum; nam-thar.*

Story (of house)   *tho.*

Stout (of men and animals)   *sha gyak-pa.*

Stout (of things)   *bom-po.*

Stove   *thab.*

Straight   *drong-po.*

Straighten, to   *drong-po so-wa.*

Straightforward (just)   *thrim-trang-po.*

Straightway   *lam-sang.*

Strain, to   *tsak-pa.*

Strainer, tea   *cha-tsha.*

Strait (narrow)   *tok-po; bu-su tok-po.*

Strange   *khye-tsha-po.*

Stranger   *chhi-mi.*

110

Strangle, to   *ke-kak tang-ne se-pa.*

Strategy   *mak-chu.*

Straw   *sem-pa.*

Strawberry (chumbi valley dialect)   *ma-lum.*

Stray, to   *lang-ka nor-wa.*

Stream   *gyuk-chhu.*

Street   *lang-ka.*

Strength   *she.*

Stretch, to   *kyang-wa.*

Strew, to (grass, etc.)   *tor-wa.*

Strewing oblation   *tor-ma.*

Strict   *tam-po; tsem-po.*

Strife   *gyam-dre.*

Strike, to (a blow)   *dung-wa.*

Strike, to (hit)   *phok-pa.*

String   *ku-pa.*

Strip, to   *shu-wa.*

Strive, to   *nying-ru che-pa.*

Stroke   *cha.*

Stroll, to   *chham-chham-la dro-wa.*

Strong (of forts, house, etc.)   *tsem-po.*

Strong (of human beings, animals etc   *she chhem-po.*

Struggle, to (wrestle)   *dzing-wa; dzing-re tang-wa.*

Stubble   *so-ma.*

Stubborn   *kyong-po.*

Student   *lap-tra.*

Stumble, to (of animals)   *tshik-pu gyap-pa.*

Stumble, to (of persons)   *kha dap-pa.*

Stupid (weak in intellect)   *kuk-pa; lem-pa.*

Sturdy   *she chhem-po.*

Stuttering   *kha-di.*

Sty   *phak-tshang.*

Style (of persons)   *gyu; ri.*

Style (of things)   *gyu-ta.*

Styles, different   *na-tsho.*

Subdue, to   *gye-wa; la khe-pa.*

Subject (of a government)   *nga-bang.*

Subjoin, to   *thu gyap-pa.*

Subjugate, to   *gye-wa; la khe-pa.*

Sublime   *yang-dze.*

Submissive (humble)   *sem-chhung-chhung*

Submit, to   *go gur-wa.*

Submit, to (a petition or report)   *bul-wa; bu-lam shu-pa.*

Subside, to (of water, flood, etc.)   *chhak-pa.*

Substance   *ngo-po; gyu.*

Substantiate, to (statement) ten-den che-pa.

Substitute tshap.

Subtility yo-gyu.

Subtle yo-chhem-po.

Subtract, to them-pa.

Succeed, to (be successful) thup-pa.

Successful, to be go thom-pa.

Succession, (descendants) ri-gyu; mi-gyu.

Succour, to ro che-pa.

Succour, s. ro.

Such din-dra.

Suck, to jip-pa.

Suckle, to o-ma ter-wa.

Suddenly lam-sang.

Suffer, to (pain) su-gyap-pa.

Suffer, to (permit) chuk-pa.

Suffer, to (endure) so-pa gom-pa.

Suffering (mental) du-nge.

Suffering (physical) su.

Sufficient, to be dang-wa; drik-pa.

Suffocated, to be u gak-pa.

Sugar che-ma ka-ra.

Sugar-candy she ka-ra.

Suicide, to commit rang-so che-pa.

Suit, to (befit) o-pa.

Suitable o-po; o-pap.

Suite khor-yo.

Sulk, to dong nak-po tem-pa.

Sullen kyong-po.

Sully, to sok-pa so-wa.

Sulphur mu-si.

Sum-up, to dom-pa.

Summer yar-ka.

Summer yar-kha.

Summit tse.

Summon, to ke tang-wa.

Sun nyi-ma.

Sunbeam nyi-me ser.

Sunday sa-nyi-ma.

Sunday za nyi-ma.

Sundry (various) mi-chik-pa.

Sunrise nyi-ma shar-ra.

Sunset nyi-ma ge-pa.

Sunstroke, to get nyi-ser phok-pa.

Superabundant ha-chang mang-po; yo-ma-sι

Superb yang-dze.

Supercilious (haughty) nyam-chhem-po; dza-kho chhem po.

Superfluous hlak-po.

Superior (rank of persons)
tho-po.

Superstition   nam-to.

Supervise, to   to-tam che-pa.

Supper   gong-mo kha-la.

Supple   nyem-po.

Supplicate, to   shu-wa.

Supplication   shu-wa.

Supply, to   drup-pa.

Support to (endure)   so-pa
gam-pa.

Support, to (nourish)   so-wa.

Support, to (prop up)   kyor-wa.

Support, to (endure) hon.
so-pa gom-pa nang-wa.

Suppose, to   sam-pa.

Supposition (opinion)   sam-pa.

Suppress, to (restrain)   kak-pa.

Suppression of urine, to suffer
from   chim-pa gak-pa.

Suppurate, to   na sak-pa.

Suprintend   to-tam che-pa.

Suprintendent   to-tam-pa.

Sure   ten-ten; thrik-thri.

Surely   nge-par.

Surety   khe-khya.

Surety, to stand   khe-kya che-pa.

Surgeon   shag-cho em-ji.

Surly   kyong-po.

Surmise, to (conjecture)   sam-pa.

Surmise, to (suspect)   tok-pa
sa-wa.

Surplus   hla-ma.

Surprise, s.   yam-tshen.

Surprise, to   yam-tshen che-pa.

Surprising   yum-tshem-po;
khye-tsha-po.

Surrender, to (abandon)   pang-wa.

Surrender, to (submit)   gop-te
shu-wa.

Surround, to   kor-ra gyap-pa.

Survey, to (look at)   ta-wa.

Suspect, to   tok-pa sa-wa.

Suspect, to, hon.   thu-to
nang-wa.

Suspend, to   kel-wa.

Suspend, to (from office)   tom-pa.

Suspense (doubt)   the-tshom.

Suspense, to be in (doubt)
the-tshom sa-wa.

Suspicion   tok-pa.

Suspicious and angry, to be
ta-chhok che-pa

Sustain, to (endure)   so-pa
gom-pa.

Sustain, to (prop)   kyor-wa.

Sustain, to (nourish)   so-wa.

wallow, to   *mi-pa.*

warm (croud)   *tsho.*

way   *wang.*

way to (govern)   *wang-che-pa.*

wear, to   *na kyel-wa.*

weat, s.   *ngu-na.*

weat, to   *ngu-na thom-pa.*

weep, to   *ke gyap-pa.*

weeper   *ke-pa; ra-gya-pa.*

weet   *ngaa-mo.*

weet-scented   *tri-ma shim-pe.*

weetheart   *nying-du.*

weetmeal   *chi-ri.*

well   *tang-wa.*

wift   *gyok-po.*

wim   *kye gyap-pa.*

wine   *phak-pa.*

wineherd   *phak-dzi.*

wing, (e.g.branch in wind)
        ling-ling che-pa.

witch   *te-cha; chang-nyu.*

woon, to   *tren-me gyel-wa.*

word   *pa-dam : sho-lang.*

symbol   *ta.*

symmetry (proportion)   *tsho.*

sympathy   *nying-je;*
        cham-nying-je.

symptom (of disease)   *na-tang.*

Syphilis   *se-mo.*

System (method)   *thap.*

T

Table   *chog-tse.*

Table-cloth   *cho-khep.*

Taciturn, to be   *kha-kha de-pa.*

Tact   *thap-khe.*

Tail   *shu-gu.*

Tailor   *tshem-pu.*

Taint (contamination)   *trip.*

Take hold of, to   *sim-pa.*

Take off   *pi-pa.*

Take out, to   *lom-pa.*

Take, to   *lem-pa.*

Take, to (carry)   *khe dro-wa.*

Take, to (conduct)   *thri dro-wa.*

Take, to (conduct)h.hon.   *thri*
        chhip-gyu nang-wa.

Take, to (forcibly)   *phok-pa.*

Tale   *drum; nam-thar.*

Talent (natural gift)   *yon-ten.*

Talented (person)   *rik-pa*
        chhem-pa.

Talisman   *hrung-nga.*

Talk (rumour)   *ke-chha; tam.*

Talk, s. (conversation)   *ke-chha.*

114

Talk, to   *lap-pa.*

Talk, to, hon.   *sung-wa.*

Tall   *suk-po ring-po.*

Tallow   *tshi-lu.*

Talon   *der-mo.*

Tame, to   *hling-po so-wa.*

Tan, to   *nye-pa.*

Tanner   *ko-wa nye-khen.*

Tap, to   *tak-ta tang-wa.*

Tape-worm   *kup-bu.*

Tape.measuring   *thak-tshe.*

Tardy   *chhi-po.*

Target   *gyam-be.*

Tarnish, to   *tsok-pa so-wa.*

Tarry, to   *gor-po che-pa.*

Tarry, to, hon.   *gor-po nang-wa.*

Tartar (on the teeth)   *so-tre.*

Task   *le-ka.*

Task, school   *yik-tshe.*

Tassel (for hat)   *tong-ku.*

Taste, s.   *tro-a.*

Taste, to   *tro-a ta-wa.*

Taunt, to   *kya-kya che-ne lap-pa.*

Tavern   *chhang-khang.*

Tax (general)   *thre, bap.*

Tax, to pay   *thre-je-wa.*

Tea   *ja.*

Tea pot   *kho-tee.*

Tea, brick of   *cha-pa-ka.*

Tea, best quality   *dru-thang.*

Tea-pot   *kho-ti.*

Tea-strainer   *cha-tsha.*

Teach, to   *lap-pa.*

Teacher   *ge-gen; lo-pon.*

Tear, s.   *mik-chhu.*

Tear, to (cloth, etc.)   *re-wa.*

Tear, to (nesh)   *kok-pa.*

Tears, to shed   *mik-chhu sher-wa.*

Tears, to shed, hon.
   chen-chhap shor-wa.

Tedious   *ka-le khak-po.*

Telegram   *lo-ku yi-ge.*

Telegraph   *cha-ku; lo-ku.*

Telephone   *kha-par.*

Telescope   *gyang-she.*

Tell, to   *lap-pa.*

Temper (passion)   *tshik-pa; khong-thro.*

Temperate (climate)   *si-tro nyom-po.*

Temperate, to be (moderate)   *tsho-sim-pa.*

Temperature   *tsha-dang.*

Tempered, bad   *ru ngar-po.*

Tempered, good   *lo-gyu ring-po.*

Tempest *lung-tshup.*

Temple *tsug-la-khang.*

Tempt, to (cheat) *go-kor tang-wa.*

Tempt, to (entice) *sem lu-pa.*

Ten *chu.*

Ten thousand *thri.*

Tenacious (obstinate) *kyong-po.*

Tenant *mi-ser; bang.*

Tender *jam-po.*

Tendon *gyu-pa.*

Tenet *chho-lu.*

Tent *gur.*

Tent-pole *kur-gyu.*

Tenth *chu-pa.*

Tepid *tron-jam.*

Term (limit) *tha.*

Terminate, to *tshar-wa.*

Terrible *she-tra tsha-po.*

Terribly *she-tra.*

Terrified, to be *she-pa.*

Terrify, to *she-tra lang-wa.*

Terrifying *she-tra tsha-po.*

Territory *sa-chha.*

Terror *she-tra.*

Test, to *tsho ta-wa.*

Testament (will) *kha-chhem.*

Testicle *lik-pa.*

Testify, to *pang-po che-pa.*

Than *le.*

Thangka *thang-ka.*

Thank you! *o ya-chung.*

Thankful, to be *trin trem-pa.*

Thanks *thu-je-chhe.*

That *te.*

That down there *ma-ki.*

That over there *pha-ki.*

That up there *ya-ki.*

That very *pha-ke-rang.*

That, just like *ta-ka-rang; ten-dra.*

Thaw, to *shu-wa.*

The, def.art. *di; te.*

Theft *ku-ma.*

Their *khom-tsho.*

Them *khon-tsho.*

Then (after that) *te-ne.*

There *te; pha-gi.*

Thermometer *tsha-trang la-ya.*

Thermos *tsha-dham.*

These *di-tsho.*

Theu *khyo; khyo-rang.*

They *khon-tsho.*

Thick (of flat objects) *thuk-po.*

Thief   *ku-ma.*

Thieve, to   *ku-ma ku-wa.*

Thigh   *le-sha.*

Thigh-bone trumpet   *kang-ling.*

Thimble   *cho-mo.*

Thin (of flat objects)   *trap-po.*

Thine   *khyo-re.*

Thing   *cha-la.*

Think, to (reflect)   *sam-lo tang-wa.*

Think, to (suppose)   *sam-pa.*

Third   *sum-pa.*

Thirdly   *sum-pa.*

Thirsty, to be   *kha kom-pa.*

Thirteen   *chug-sum.*

Thirteenth   *chuk-sum-pa.*

Thirtieth   *sum-chu-pa.*

Thirty   *sum-chu.*

This   *di.*

This very   *ta-ka-rang.*

Thither   *te.*

Thorn   *tsher-ma.*

Thorough, to be (complete)   *phu khyo-wa.*

Thoroughly   *be-te.*

Those   *te-tsho.*

Though   *ne; kyang; rung; na-yang.*

Thought (intention)   *ton-ta.*

Thought (opinion)   *sam-pa.*

Thousand   *tong-thra.*

Thousand, hundred   *bum.*

Thrash, to   *yo-ma-su dung-wa.*

Thread,   *ku-pa.*

Threaten, to   *dzik-dzik tang-wa.*

Three   *sum.*

Thresh, to (corn)   *dung-wa.*

Threshhold   *them-pa.*

Thrice   *tshar-sum.*

Thriving   *yang-chhem-po.*

Throat   *mig-pa.*

Throne   *shuk-thri.*

Throng (of men)   *mi-tsho.*

Through (by the agency of)   *gyu-ne.*

Throw at, to   *shu-wa.*

Throw, to   *gyap-pa; yuk-pa.*

Thumb   *kang-pay the-po.*

Thunder   *druk-ke.*

Thunder, to   *druk-ke kyom-pa.*

Thunderbolt   *tho.*

Thursday   *sa-phur-pu.*

Thursday   *za pa-sang.*

Thus   *din-dre; ta-ka-se.*

Thwart, to   *kak-pa.*

Tibet   *po.*

Tibetan   *po-pa.*

Tickle, to   *i-ku lu-ku sak-pa.*

Tidings   *ne-tshu; sang-gyu.*

Tie, to   *dam-pa.*

Tiffin   *nyin-kung kha-la.*

Tiger   *ta.*

Tight   *tam-po.*

Till   *thuk-la; par-tu.*

Till, to   *mom-pa gyap-pa.*

Tillage   *so-nam.*

Tiller, s. (one who tills)   *mom-pa gyang-khen; thon-khe.*

Timber   *shing-chha.*

Time   *tu; tu-tsho.*

Time, at the present (now-a-days)   *te-ring sang teng-sang.*

Time, to pass the   *go-khor-wa.*

Tin   *sha-ka.*

Tinder   *pa-a.*

Tip (gratuity)   *chhang-ring.*

Tip (point)   *tse.*

Tipsy   *rap-si.*

Tired   *ka-le khak-po.*

Tired, to be   *thang-chhe-pa.*

Tiresome (tedious)   *ka-le khak-po.*

Titan (demi-god)   *hla-ma-yin.*

Title   *ko-sa : ko-ne.*

To (as far as)   *par-la.*

To (in presence of a person)   *tsa-la*

To-day   *te-ring.*

To-morrow   *sang-nyi.*

To-morrow morning   *sang-sho nga-po.*

To-night   *to-gong gong-mo.*

Tobacco   *tha-ma.*

Tobacco pipe   *kang-sa.*

Tobacco pouch   *tha-khu.*

Today   *dhe-ring.*

Toe   *kang-pe dzuk-ku.*

Toe, the big   *kang-pe the-po.*

Together (jointly)   *nyam-drel.*

Together with, prep.   *tang-nyam-tu.*

Toilet   *sang-cho.*

Toilsome   *ka-le khak-po.*

Token   *ta.*

Tolerate to (permit)   *chuk-pa.*

Tolerate, to (endure)   *so-pa gom-pa.*

Tom-cat   *pho-shim.*

Tomb   *tur-khung.*

Tomorrow   *sang-nyin.*

Tone   *dang.*

Tongue   *che.*

Tongue (dialect)   *ke-lu.*

Too (very)   *ha-chang.*

Too few, to be   *nyung trak-pa.*

Too little, to be   *chhung trak-pa.*

Too many, to be   *mang trak-pa.*

Too much, to be   *hlak-pa.*

Too, conj.   *yang.*

Tool   *lak-chha.*

Tooth   *so.*

Tooth brush   *so-troo.*

Tooth paste   *so-men.*

Tooth, lower   *me-so.*

Tooth, front   *dun-so.*

Tooth, molar   *dram-so.*

Tooth, upper   *ya-so.*

Toothless   *so-me.*

Top (summit)   *tse.*

Torch   *pem-bar.*

Torment, to (annoy)   *khong-thro lang-wa.*

Torn, to be   *re-wa.*

Tortoise   *ru-be.*

Tortuous   *kyo-kyo.*

Torture (agony of mind)   *du-nge.*

Total, in the   *dom-ne.*

Totter, to   *khyor-ne dro-wa.*

Touch, to   *thuk-pa; chhang-wa.*

Towards   *chhok-la; ngo-la.*

Towel   *a-chor.*

Town   *trong-khyer.*

Toy   *tse-mo tse-ya.*

Track (footprint)   *kang-je.*

Track (path)   *lang-ka.*

Tract (of country)   *lung-pa.*

Trade, to   *tshong-gyap-pa.*

Trade, s.   *tshong.*

Trader   *tshong-pa.*

Traduce, to   *me-ra tang-wa.*

Traffic   *tshong.*

Train, to (teach)   *lap-pa.*

Trammel s. (hindrance)   *kak-chha.*

Trammel, to   *kak-pa.*

Tramp, s (loafer)   *gyeng-kham kor-khen.*

Trample, to   *kang-pe dzi-wa.*

Tranquil (of places)   *kha-ku sim-pu.*

Transfer, to   *je-wa.*

Transgress, to   *dik-pa sak-pa.*

Transgression   *dik-pa.*

Translate, to   *gyur-wa.*

Transmigrate, to   *kye-wa pho-pa.*

Transmigration, cycle of   *si-pa khor-lo.*

Transport   *khe-ma.*

Transport, to   *ta-u kyel-wa.*

Trap   *nyi.*

Travail (child-birth)   *kye-su.*

Traveller   *dru-pa.*

Tray   *shing-thro.*

Tread, to   *kang-le thep-pa.*

Treasure, s.   *kang-juk.*

Treasurer   *chhan-dzo.*

Treasury   *ngu-khang.*

Treat, s. (feast)   *drom-po.*

Treat, to (entertain)   *drom-po tang-wa.*

Treatment   *men-cho.*

Treaty   *chhing-yi.*

Tree   *shing-dong.*

Tremble, to (of animate beings)   *dar-wa.*

Tremble, to (of inanimate things)   *thruk-pa.*

Trench   *tong.*

Trial (experiment)   *ship-chha.*

Triangle   *sur-sum.*

Tribe   *mi-gyu; ri-gyu.*

Tribunal   *thrim-khang.*

Tribute   *thre; bap.*

Trick (deceit)   *go-kor.*

Trickle, to   *thik-pa gyap-pa.*

Tricky (artful)   *chang-po.*

Trident   *kha-tam.*

Trifling, (matter), adj.   *ton-ne chhung chhung.*

Trigger   *kam-pa.*

Tripod   *kung-sum.*

Trivial   *ton-ne chhung-chhung.*

Troop   *mak-pung.*

Trouble   *ka-le.*

Troublesome (of persons)   *cha-sing-po.*

Troublesome (of things)   *ka-le khak-po.*

Trousers   *ko-thung; tor-ma.*

True   *ngo-tho; ngo-ne.*

Truly   *ngo-ne.*

Trumpet   *tung.*

Trumpet, thigh bone   *kang-ling.*

Trunk (box)   *gam.*

Trunk (of elephant)   *chhu-do.*

Trunk (of tree)   *dong-po.*

Trunk, iron (box)   *cha-gam.*

Trust (confidence)   *lo-te.*

Trust, to   *lo ke-wa.*

Trustworthy   *lo khe-ra.*

Truth   *ngo-tho; ngo-ne.*

Try, to (make effort)   *nying-ru che-pa.*

Try, to (test)   *tsho ta-wa; khok-pa lem-pa.*

Tuesday   *sa mik-mar.*

Tuesday   *za mig-maa*

Tumble, to   *gye-wa.*

Tumble, to (from a height)   *sak-pa.*

Tumour   *nyem-bur.*

Tumult   *gyam-dre; thruk-pa.*

Tune   *dang.*

Turban   *le-to.*

Turbid   *nyok-po.*

Turf   *pang.*

Turkistan   *hor lung-pa; hor-yu.*

Turn back to front, to   *kha-chho lok-pa.*

Turn round, to   *khor-wa.*

Turn upside down, to   *go-shu lok-pa; a-lo gyap-pa.*

Turnip   *nyung-ma.*

Turquoise   *yu.*

Turquoise (worn in head-dress)   *yu.*

Turquoise earring   *si-yu.*

Tusk   *chhe-wa.*

Tutelary deity   *yi-dam.*

Tutor   *ge-gen.*

Twelfth   *chu-nyi-pa.*

Twelve   *chung-nyi.*

Twentieth   *nyi-shu-pa.*

Twenty   *nyi-snu.*

Twice   *tshar-nyi.*

Twilight, at   *sa rip-ne.*

Twin   *tshe-ma.*

Twine   *ku-pa.*

Twist, to   *drim-pa.*

Two   *nyee*

U

Udder   *sho.*

Ugly   *kha-do nye-po.*

Ulcer   *shu-wa.*

Ultimate   *shuk-sho.*

Umbrage, to take   *tsher-wa.*

Umbrella   *nyi-du.*

Unable, to be   *mi thup-pa.*

Unavailing, to be (useless)   *phen mi thok-pa.*

Unbearable (pain)   *gong mi thup-pa.*

Unbiassed   *thrim trang-po.*

Unbreakable, to be   *chhak-gyu me-pa.*

Unbridled (licentious)   *do-chha chhem-po.*

Unceasing   *gyun-chhe-gyu me-pa.*

Unceasingly   *nam-gyun; tu-gyun.*

Uncertain, to be   *the-tshom sa-wa.*

Uncertainty	*the-tshom.*
Unchaste	*do-chha chhem-po.*
Uncivil	*drik-me.*
Uncle, maternal	*shang-shang.*
Unclean	*tsok-pa.*
Unclothed	*mar-hrang-nga.*
Uncommon (rare)	*kom-po.*
Unconquerable	*la...mi kha-wa.*
Undaunted	*lo-kho chhem-po.*
Undefined	*tem-po me-pa.*
Under	*o-la.*
Understand, to	*she-pa; ha-ke-wa.*
Understand, to, h.hon.	*gong-pa tok-pa.*
Understanding	*rik-pa.*
Undo, to (nullify)	*me-pa sa-wa.*
Undo, to (untie)	*trol-wa; hik-pa.*
Undress, to	*pi-pa.*
Unendurable (pain)	*gong mi thup-pa.*
Uneven, to be	*nyom-pa me-pa.*
Unfasten, to (button, etc.)	*pi-pa.*
Unfasten, to (knot, etc.)	*shik-pa.*
Unfit	*o-po me-pa.*
Unfortunate	*so-de me-pa; so-de chhung-chhung.*
Unfortunate, to be	*so-de me-pa.*
Unhappy, to be	*kyi-po me-pa.*

Uniform (alike)	*chik-pa; dran-da.*
Uniform (dress)	*mak-chhe.*
Unimportant	*ton-ta chhung-chhung.*
Unintelligible	*mi ko-wa.*
Uninterrupted	*gyun-chhe-gyu me-pa.*
Uninterruptedly	*nam-gyun; tu-gyun.*
Unite, to	*thu-gyap-pa.*
Unitedly (jointly)	*nyam-drel.*
Universal (all)	*tshang-ma tham-che; gang-kha; ru.*
Unlawful	*thrim-me.*
Unlearned	*yon-ten me-pa.*
Unless, with verb "to do"	*ma che-na.*
Unlimited	*tsho me-pa.*
Unloose, to (dress, etc.)	*pi-pa.*
Unlucky	*so-de me-pa : so-de chhung-chhung.*
Unlucky, to be	*so-de me-pa.*
Unmarried, man	*pho-hrang-nga.*
Unmerciful, to be	*nying-je me-pa.*
Unmerciful, to be, hon.	*thuk-je me-pa.*
Unprejudiced (of judge)	*thrim trang-po.*

Unprofitable, to be *phen thok-pa.*

Unreasonable *ton-me.*

Unrelenting, to be *nying-je me-pa.*

Unserviceable, to be *phen mi thok-pa.*

Unsettled (indefinite) *tem-po me-pa.*

Untensils *lak-chha.*

Untie, to *trol-wa; shik-pa.*

Until *thuk-la.*

Untruth *ham-pa; kyak-dzun.*

Unusual (extraordinary) *yam-tshem-po; khye-tsha-po.*

Unusual (rare) *kom-po.*

Unwell, to be *de-po me-pa; suk-po thang-po me-pa*

Up *ya.*

Up to *thuk-la.*

Up-hill *kyen.*

Upon *teng-la; gang-la.*

Upper *ya-ki.*

Upper arm *lak-nya.*

Upper tooth *ya-so.*

Upraid, to *she-she tang-wa.*

Upright (erect) *kye-re.*

Upright (moral, virtuous) *tshun-den.*

Upshot *nying-po.*

Upstairs *yap-tho.*

Urge, to (insist) *u-tshu che-pa.*

Urgent (work) *thre-thre che go-ya.*

Urine *chim-pa.*

Urine, to discharge *chim-pa tang-wa.*

Urn (containing ashes of dead lama) *ku-dung.*

Us *nga-tsho.*

Usage *luk-so.*

Use (custom) *luk-so.*

Use, to (employ) *ko-wa.*

Use, to be of *phen thok-pa.*

Use, to be of hon. *thu-phen so-wa.*

Used to, to be *kom-pa.*

Used to, to become *kom-song-wa.*

Used up, to be *dzok-pa.*

Useful, to be *phen thok-pa.*

Useless, to be *phen mi thok-pa.*

Usually *phe-chhe.*

Usurp, to *throk-pa.*

Utensils *thab-chhey.*

Utter, to (speak) *lap-pa.*

Uttorly (used negatively) *be-te; khyon-ne.*

V

Vacant *tong-pa.*

Vaccine lymph   *thor-pe-men.*

Vacillate, to   *the-tshom so-wa.*

Vacillation   *the-tshom.*

Vagina   *tu.*

Vagrant   *gyeng-kham kor-khen.*

Vague   *tem-po me-pa.*

Vain   *rang-to tsha-po.*

Valiant   *nying-chhem-po.*

Valley   *rong; lung-pa.*

Valorous   *nying-chhem-po.*

Valuable   *tsa chhem-po.*

Value, s.   *kong.*

Value, hon.   *ja-kong.*

Valueless   *kong-me.*

Vanish, to   *ye-wa.*

Vanity   *rang-to.*

Vanquish, to   *gye-wa; la khe-pa.*

Vanquished, to be   *pham-pa.*

Vapour   *lang-pa.*

Variable, to be   *tem-po...me-pa.*

Variation (difference) *khye; he-pa.*

Variety   *khye; he-pa.*

Various   *mi chik-pa; min dra-wa.*

Various kinds of   *na-tsho.*

Vase   *pum-pa.*

Vase, hon.   *chha-pum.*

Vast   *gya-chhem-po.*

Vaunt, to   *rang-to che-pa.*

Veal   *pe-pe sha.*

Vegetable   *tshe.*

Vegetable drug   *ngo-men.*

Vegetable garden   *tshe yang-tse.*

Vein   *tsa.*

Velveteen   *pu-ma.*

Venerable (title)   *je-tsun.*

Venerate, to   *nyen-kur che-pa.*

Veneration   *nyen-kur.*

Vengeance   *dra-len.*

Vengeance, to take   *dra-len lem-pa.*

Venial (trivial)   *ton-ne chhung-chhung.*

Venison   *sha-ki sha.*

Venom (poison)   *tu.*

Venom (spite)   *no-sem.*

Venture, to   *nu-pa.*

Venturesome   *kha-me mik-me.*

Verandah (roofed in)   *tho-yang.*

Verbal   *khe.*

Verbally   *kha-ne.*

Verdict (judgment)   *che-tsham; thra-ma.*

Vermilion   *tshe; gyam-tshe.*

Vermin   *bu.*

Verse	*tshik-che.*
Vertebrae	*ge-tshi.*
Vertigo	*pu-lung go-khor.*
Very	*ha-chang.*
Very good	*yag-po zhe-daa.*
Vessel (for water)	*chhu-no.*
Vessel (ship)	*tru.*
Vex, to	*khong-thro lang-wa.*
Vexed to be	*tshik-pa sa-wa.*
Viands	*kha-la; to.*
Vibrate, to	*thruk-pa.*
Vice	*dik-pa.*
Vicinity	*nye-khor.*
Vicious	*ngem-po.*
Victorious, to be	*gye-wa.*
Victuals	*kha-la; to.*
View (opinion)	*sam-pa.*
View (purpose)	*ton-ta.*
View, to	*thong-wa; ta-wa.*
Vigorous	*she chhem-po.*
Vigour	*she.*
Vile (dirty)	*tsok-pa.*
Vilification	*me-ra.*
Vilify, to	*me-ra tang-wa.*
Village	*dong-seb.*
Villager	*trong-pa.*
Villain	*dzap-chhen.*
Vine	*aun-drum-shing.*
Vinegar	*tshu-u.*
Violence (force)	*wang-yo.*
Violence, to show	*wang-yo che-pa.*
Violet (colour)	*gun-drum do.*
Virgin	*pu-mo.*
Virtue	*ge-wa.*
Virtuous	*tshun-den.*
Virus (poison)	*tu.*
Visible, to be	*thong-wa.*
Vision (spectre)	*dong-dre; dre.*
Visit, to (a person)	*char-wa.*
Vituperate, to	*me-ra tang-wa.*
Vituperation	*me-ra.*
Vocabulary	*ming-dzo.*
Vocation	*le-ka.*
Vocation, hon.	*chha-le.*
Voice	*ke; dra.*
Void (empty)	*tong-pa.*
Volume (of book)	*po-ti.*
Vomit	*kyug-pa.*
Voracious (gluttonous)	*tro-chhem-po.*
Vouch, to	*khe-khya che-pa.*
Voucher (guarantor)	*khe-khya che-khen.*
Vow (religious)	*tam-cha.*

Vowels   *yang.*

Vulgar (of language, opp.to hon.)
          she-sa me-pa.

W

Wag (jester)   *u-khor shu-khen.*

Wag, to (dog's tail)   *ri-ri che-pa.*

Wag, to (shake)   *yuk-yu che-pa.*

Wager   *gyen.*

Wager, to   *gyen shak-pa.*

Wages   *la; pho.*

Waggish   *ge-mo tro-po.*

Waggon   *shing-ta khor-lo.*

Waist   *ke-pa.*

Waist band   *ke-ra.*

Waistcoat   *khen-jar.*

Wait on, to   *kun-dun-la char-wa.*

Wait, to   *ngu-wa.*

Wait, to, v.t.   *gu de-pa.*

Wake, to   *nyi se-pa.*

Walk, to   *kang-thang la dro-wa.*

Walk, to (of horses)   *kom-pa dro-wa.*

Walk, to take a   *chham-chham la dro-wa.*

Wall   *tsik-pa.*

Walnut   *tar-ka.*

Wan   *kar-po kar-kyang.*

Wander, to (go astray)   *lam-ka nor-wa.*

Wander, to (stroll)   *chham-chham la dro-wa.*

Want, to (wish)   *do-pa che-pa.*

Want, to (need)   *go-wa.*

Wanton   *do-chha chhem-po.*

War   *ma.*

Wardrobe   *tu-lo luk-se gam.*

Wares   *tshong-ya.*

Warm   *tro-po.*

Warn, to   *lap-cha che-pa.*

Warn, to, hon.   *lap-cha nang-wa.*

Warp, s. (of loom)   *gyu.*

Warrant, to(guarantee)   *khe-khya che-pa.*

Warrant, to (authorize)   *wang tre-pa.*

Warrantly   *khe-khya.*

Warrior   *ma-mi.*

Wart, s.   *men.*

Wash, to   *thru-pa.*

Wasp   *tuk-drang.*

Waste, to   *tor-wa.*

Watch, to   *mik ta-wa.*

Watch, to (guard)   *sung-wa.*

Watch, s. *chhu-tsho khor-lo.*

Watchman *mik-ta-khen; sung-khen.*

Water *chu.*

Water (for drinking) *thung-ya-ki chhu.*

Water-mill *chhu-kho.*

Water-vessel *chhu-no.*

Waterfall *pap-chhu.*

Wave, to *yuk-yu che-pa.*

Wave, s. *ba-lap.*

Waver, to *the-tshom sa-wa.*

Wavering *the-tshom.*

Wax, sealing *la-chha.*

Way (highway) *gya-lam.*

Way (manner) *thap.*

Way (road) *lang-ka.*

We *nga-tsho; nga-rang-tsho.*

Weak (in muscle) *she chhung-chhùng.*

Weak (prone to illness) *suk-po chong-po.*

Weakminded *kuk-pa; lem-pa.*

Wealthy *chhuk-po; cha-la chhem-po.*

Weapon *tshon-chha.*

Wear, to *kom-pa.*

Weariness *ngel.*

Wearisome *ka-le khak-po.*

Weary, to be *thang chhe-pa.*

Weasel *tre-mong.*

Weather *nam.*

Weave, to *tha thak-pa.*

Weaver *thang-khen.*

Web *tha.*

Wed, to (take husband) *mak-pa lang-wa.*

Wed, to (take wife) *no-ma lem-pa.*

Wedding *chhang-sa.*

Wedge *ke-u.*

Wednesday *sa-hlak-pa.*

Weed *tsa-ngen.*

Weed, to *yur-ma gyap-pa.*

Week *dun-thra.*

Weep *ngu-wa.*

Weft *pun.*

Weigh, to *kyak-pa.*

Weigh, to (consider) *sam-lo tang-wa.*

Weight *yang-chi.*

Weighty (heavy) *ji-po.*

Welcome *chaa-phe nang.*

Welcome ! *chha-phe nang-chung.*

Well, to be (in health) *suk-po de-po yo-pa.*

Well, s. *throm-pa.*

Well-behaved *ya-rap.*

Well-known (celebrated) *ke-tra chhem-po.*

Well-known (celebrated) hon. *tshen-nyen-ta chhem-po.*

Well-modelled *ko-pa to-po.*

Wenesday *za lhag-pa.*

West *nup.*

Westward *nup-ngo; nup-chho.*

Wet *lom-pa.*

Wet, to *bang-wa.*

Wether *luk-pho.*

What, interr.and rel. *ka-re.*

Whatever it is *ka-re yin-ne.*

Wheat *tro.*

Wheat-flour *tro-ship.*

Wheedle, to (for bad object) *lu-wa.*

Wheedle, to (for good object) *lap-cha gyap-pa.*

Wheel *khor-lo.*

When, interr. *ka-tu.*

When, rel. *tu.*

Whence *ka-ne.*

Whenever *ka-tu...yang.*

Where, interr.and rel. *ka-pa.*

Wherever *ka-pa...yang.*

Whet, to *dar-wa.*

Whether *ne.*

Whetstone *dar-do.*

Which of them *ka-ki.*

Which, interr. and rel. *ka-re.*

While, adv. *tu.*

Whip *te-cha.*

Whirlwind *lung-tshup.*

Whiskers, *gya-u.*

Whisper, s. *shap-shop.*

Whisper, to *shap-shop lap-pa.*

Whistle a tune, to *si-lu tang-wa.*

Whistle, to *si gyap-pa.*

White *kar-po.*

Whitewash *sa-kar; kar-tsi.*

Whither *ka-pa.*

Who *su.*

Whoever (you, he, etc.) be *su yin-ne.*

Whole *tshang-ma; tham-che; gang-kha.*

Wholly (used negatively) *be-te; khyon-ne.*

Whore *shang-tshong-ma.*

Why, interr. *ka-re ton-la.*

Wick *dong-re.*

Wicked *ngem-po.*

Wickedness *dik-pa.*

Wide *shang-chhem-po.*

128

Widow (term of reproach) *yuk-sa-ma.*

Width *shang.*

Wife *kyi-men.*

Wild animal *ri-ta.*

Wilderness *che-thang.*

Wile, s. *go-kor.*

Will, s. (testament) *kha-chhem.*

Will, s. (testament), hon. *she-chhem.*

Will, s. (wish) *do-pa.*

Willing, to be *do-pa yo-pa.*

Willow *chang-ma.*

Wily *chang-po.*

Win, to (conquer) *gyel-wa.*

Win, to (obtain) *jor-wa; thop-pa.*

Wind *hlak-pa; lung.*

Wind, to *dril-wa.*

Winding *kuo-kyo.*

Window *gi-khung.*

Window-grating *thra-ma.*

Wine (beer) *chhang.*

Wing *shok-pa.*

Wink, to *mik thrap-thrap che-pa.*

Winter *gun-ka.*

Winter *gung-kha.*

Wintry (cold) *trang-mo; si-po.*

Wipe out, to (efface) *sup-pa.*

Wipe, to *chhi-pa.*

Wire *cha-ku.*

Wireless telegraphy *cha-ku me-pe tar.*

Wisdom *lo-tro.*

Wise (skilful) *khe-po.*

Wish *do-pa.*

Wish, to *do-pa che-pa.*

Wit, (intellect) *lo-tro.*

Witchcraft *thu.*

With (together with) *tang-nyam-tu.*

With regard to *ton-la; kor-la.*

Withdraw, to, v.i. (retreat) *chhi-lo gyap-pa.*

Wither, to *nyi-pa.*

Withhold, to (restrain) *kak-pa.*

Within *nang-la.*

Without (opp. to within) *chhi-lo-la.*

Without (opp.to "with") *me-pa.*

Withstand, to (restrain) *kak-pa.*

Witless *kuk-pa; lem-pa.*

Witness *pang-po.*

Witness, to *pang-po che-pa.*

Woe *du-nge; sem-thre.*

Wolf	*chang-ku.*
Woman	*kyi-men.*
Womb	*pu-no.*
Wonder	*yam-tshen.*
Wonder, to	*khye tshar-wa.*
Wonderful	*yam-tshem-po;* *khye-tsha-po.*
Wondrous	*yam-tshem-po;* *khye-tsha-po.*
Wood	*shing.*
Wooden	*shing-ki.*
Woof, s. (of loom)	*pun.*
Wool	*pe.*
Woolen	*pe-kyi.*
Woolen cloth	*nam-pu.*
Word	*tshi.*
Word, to give one's promise	*khe-lang-wa.*
Work	*le-ka.*
Work, to	*le-ka che-pa.*
Work, to be, occupied with	*tre-wa yo-pa.*
World	*dzam-pu-ling; jik-ten.*
Worm	*bu.*
Worry, to, v.i.	*sem-thre che-pa.*
Worry, to, v.t. (vex)	*khong-thro lang-wa.*

Worship, to (extempore prayers)	*mo-lam tap-pa.*
Worship, to (written prayers)	*khan-don che-pa.*
Worst	*duk-sho.*
Worst of, to get the	*pham-pa.*
Worth	*kong.*
Worth, to be	*kong-che-pa.*
Worthless (valueless)	*kong-me.*
Worthy	*o-po.*
Wound, to	*ma so-wa.*
Wound, s.	*ma.*
Wound, to, hon.	*ma so-wa nang-wa.*
Wrangle, to	*gyam-dre gyap-pa.*
Wrap, to	*dril-wa.*
Wrath	*tshik-pa; khong-thro.*
Wrathful, to be	*tshik-pa sa-wa; khong-thro sa-wa.*
Wrest, to	*throk-pa.*
Wrestle, to	*dzing-re tang-wa.*
Wretched (bad)	*duk-ru.*
Wretchedness	*dung-nge; sem-thre.*
Wring, to (twist)	*drim-pa.*
Wring, to, (twist), hon.	*drim-pa nang-wa.*
Wrinkle (on face)	*nye-ma.*
Wrist	*lag-tshig.*

Write, to   *tri-pa.*

Writer (author)   *tsom-khen.*

Writer (clerk)   *trung-yi.*

Wrong (crime), to commit   *thrim gel-wa.*

Wrong, adj. (incorrect)   *ma...tak-pa.*

Wrong, s. (error)   *nor.*

X

Xylograph, to make a   *shing-ko gyap-pa.*

Y

Yak   *ya.*

Yak's meat   *tshak-sha.*

Yak, wild   *drong.*

Yak, half-breed with ordinary cattle   *dzo.*

Yak-dung   *cho.*

Yama   *shin-je chho-gye.*

Yap, to   *chhang-wa.*

Yard, court   *go-ra.*

Yarn   *hring-ku.*

Yawn, to   *a-tong gyap-pa.*

Year   *lo.*

Year before last   *shi-nyi.*

Year, last   *da-nyi.*

Year, next   *chhi-lo; sang-po.*

Year, this   *ta-lo.*

Year, first four months of a   *da-to.*

Year, last four months of a   *da-me.*

Year, middle four months of a   *da-kyi.*

Yearn for, to   *trem-pa.*

Yeast (for bread)   *chhi-men.*

Yell, to (of children crying)   *ngu-wa*

Yell, to (of dogs)   *duk-ke gyap-pa.*

Yellow   *ser-po.*

Yellow, dark   *nyuk-se.*

Yelp, to (of dogs)   *chhang-wa.*

Yes   *la-si; la.*

Yes   *rey, yin, dhoo.*

Yes, hon.   *la-la-si; la-ong.*

Yesterday   *khe-sa.*

Yesterday evening   *dang-gong.*

Yet, adv. (in addition)   *tan-do; ta-rung.*

Yet, conj. (nevertheless)   *yin-ne; yin-kyang; yin-na-yang.*

Yield, to (forego)   *pang-wa.*

Yield, to (give)   *ter-wa.*

Yield, to (admit)   *khe-lem-pa.*

Yield, to (surrender)   *go gur-wa.*

Yielding (flexible)   *nyem-po.*

Yoke (for oxen)   *nya-shing.*

Yolk   *ser-gong; ser-trin.*

Yonder   *pha-gi.*

You   *khyo, khyo-rang.*

Young   *shom-pa; lo shon-shon.*

Your   *khyo-re.*

Youthful   *shom-pa; lo shon-shon.*

Z

Zeal   *nying-ru.*

Zealous   *nyin-ru chhem-po.*

Zealous, to be   *nying-ru che-pa.*

Zealously   *nying-ru che-ne.*

Zero   *le-kor.*

Zigzag   *lam-kyo.*